Taxes and Capital Formation

A National Bureau
of Economic Research
Project Report

Taxes and Capital Formation

Edited by **Martin Feldstein**

The University of Chicago Press

Chicago and London

Martin Feldstein is the George F. Baker Professor of
Economics at Harvard University and president of the National
Bureau of Economic Research. He is the author of *Inflation, Tax
Rules, and Capital Formation,* and editor of *The American
Economy in Transition, Behavioral Simulation Methods in Tax
Policy Analysis,* and *The Effects of Taxation on Capital
Accumulation,* all published by the University of Chicago Press.

The University of Chicago Press, Chicago 60637
The University of Chicago Press, Ltd., London

Library of Congress Cataloging-in-Publication Data

Taxes and capital formation.

   (A National Bureau of Economic Research
project report)
   Includes index.
   1. Taxation—United States.   2. Saving and
investment—United States.   3. Taxation.
4. Saving and investment.   I. Feldstein, Martin S.
II. Series.
HJ2381.T395   1987   336.2′00973   87-5898
ISBN 0-226-24079-7

Relation of the Directors to the
Work and Publications of the
National Bureau of Economic Research

1. The object of the National Bureau of Economic Research is to ascertain and to present to the public important economic facts and their interpretation in a scientific and impartial manner. The Board of Directors is charged with the responsibility of ensuring that the work of the National Bureau is carried on in strict conformity with this object.

2. The President of the National Bureau shall submit to the Board of Directors, or to its Executive Committee, for their formal adoption all specific proposals for research to be instituted.

3. No research report shall be published by the National Bureau until the President has sent each member of the Board a notice that a manuscript is recommended for publication and that in the President's opinion it is suitable for publication in accordance with the principles of the National Bureau. Such notification will include an abstract or summary of the manuscript's content and a response form for use by those Directors who desire a copy of the manuscript for review. Each manuscript shall contain a summary drawing attention to the nature and treatment of the problem studied, the character of the data and their utilization in the report, and the main conclusions reached.

4. For each manuscript so submitted, a special committee of the Directors (including Directors Emeriti) shall be appointed by majority agreement of the President and Vice Presidents (or by the Executive Committee in case of inability to decide on the part of the President and Vice Presidents), consisting of three Directors selected as nearly as may be one from each general division of the Board. The names of the special manuscript committee shall be stated to each Director when notice of the proposed publication is submitted to him. It shall be the duty of each member of the special manuscript committee to read the manuscript. If each member of the manuscript committee signifies his approval within thirty days of the transmittal of the manuscript, the report may be published. If at the end of that period any member of the manuscript committee withholds his approval, the President shall then notify each member of the Board, requesting approval or disapproval of publication, and thirty days additional shall be granted for this purpose. The manuscript shall then not be published unless at least a majority of the entire Board who shall have voted on the proposal within the time fixed for the receipt of votes shall have approved.

5. No manuscript may be published, though approved by each member of the special manuscript committee, until forty-five days have elapsed from the transmittal of the report in manuscript form. The interval is allowed for the receipt of any memorandum of dissent or reservation, together with a brief statement of his reasons, that any member may wish to express; and such memorandum of dissent or reservation shall be published with the manuscript if he so desires. Publication does not, however, imply that each member of the Board has read the manuscript, or that either members of the Board in general or the special committee have passed on its validity in every detail.

6. Publications of the National Bureau issued for informational purposes concerning the work of the Bureau and its staff, or issued to inform the public of activities of Bureau staff, and volumes issued as a result of various conferences involving the National Bureau shall contain a specific disclaimer noting that such publication has not passed through the normal review procedures required in this resolution. The Executive Committee of the Board is charged with review of all such publications from time to time to ensure that they do not take on the character of formal research reports of the National Bureau, requiring formal Board approval.

7. Unless otherwise determined by the Board or exempted by the terms of paragraph 6, a copy of this resolution shall be printed in each National Bureau publication.

(Resolution adopted October 25, 1926, as revised through September 30, 1974)

Contents

Acknowledgments

This volume presents seven relatively nontechnical papers that were prepared as part of a research project by the National Bureau of Economic Research (NBER) on the effects of taxation on capital accumulation. Brief summaries of seven additional studies are also included in the volume. The volume is designed to distribute the results of the NBER's research beyond the usual audience of professional economists and policy specialists. As part of that same effort, the seven papers in this volume were presented at a conference for government and corporate officials in Washington, D.C., on 28 May 1986.

Technical versions of the fourteen studies described here are being published separately in *The Effects of Taxation on Capital Accumulation*, edited by Martin Feldstein (NBER volume published by the University of Chicago Press, 1987). The NBER research on taxation and capital accumulation has been discussed at regular meetings of the bureau's tax program and at special meetings focused on this project.

The collaborative research in this project is made possible by the ongoing activities of the NBER's tax program under the guidance of program director David F. Bradford. National Bureau Directors Andrew Brimmer, Walter W. Heller, and James L. Pierce reviewed the entire manuscript. National Bureau staff members Mark Fitz-Patrick, Deborah Mankiw, Kathi Smith, Annie Spillane, Gail Swett, and Kirsten Foss Davis contributed to the overall effort.

Introduction

Martin Feldstein

It has long been recognized that there is an important effect of capital accumulation on productivity and economic growth. In fact, more than fifty years ago the pioneering studies of capital accumulation that were done at the National Bureau of Economic Research by Nobel laureate Simon Kuznets began the process of developing quantitative knowledge about capital formation and its link to economic performance.

In the years since Kuznets began his work, many other researchers at the NBER have studied capital formation. In the 1950s, Milton Friedman and Raymond Goldsmith made important contributions to the subject. The list of researchers and the range of issues studied grew rapidly in the 1960s and 1970s.

The NBER is currently engaged in several related studies of the accumulation and financing of capital in the United States. One of these is a study of the effects of taxation on capital accumulation, including the effects on saving, risk taking, and corporate investment in the United States and abroad. The papers presented in this volume summarize seven of the individual research projects within that study.

Longer technical reports on these research projects will appear in a separate volume, *The Effects of Taxation on Capital Accumulation*, edited by me. That volume will also contain technical reports on seven additional studies that are summarized more briefly in the second part of the current volume.

We hope that these summary papers will be of interest to a wide audience of policy officials and staff, members of the business community, and others who are concerned about the effects of taxation on capital formation. In keeping with the NBER's tradition, these papers do not make any policy recommendations. Even when the researcher is convinced that a particular type of tax change will have an undesirable effect on capital formation, he or she does not offer an overall evaluation of any of the recent tax proposals because the effect on capital formation is only one of many criteria by which the desirability of a tax proposal should be judged.

A researcher might conclude, for example, that eliminating the investment tax credit would reduce investment in equipment but might nevertheless favor doing so because the revenue raised in that way could be used to help the poor by raising the zero-bracket amount or to stimulate work effort by reducing personal marginal tax rates. The papers in this volume make no attempt to assess these other aspects of the recent tax proposals and therefore should not and do not make any recommendations with respect to the alternative policy proposals.

The emphasis in these studies is on developing a better understanding of how the economy works and how specific policies would affect particular aspects of the economy. We hope that these analyses will contribute to the formulation of better economic policy in the years ahead.

I   Individual Research Projects

1   Individual Retirement Accounts and Saving

David A. Wise

Individual retirement accounts (IRAs) were established in 1974 as part of the Employee Retirement Income Security Act to encourage employees not covered by private pension plans to save for retirement. The Economic Recovery Tax Act of 1981 extended the availability of IRAs to all employees and raised the contribution limit. The legislation emphasized the need to enhance the economic well-being of future retirees and the need to increase national saving. Now any employee with earnings above $2,000 can contribute $2,000 to an IRA account each year. An employed person and a nonworking spouse can contribute a total of $2,250, while a married couple who are both working can contribute $2,000 each. Recent tax proposals have contemplated substantial increases in the limits (the current House bill is an exception). The tax on the principal and interest is deferred until money is withdrawn from the account. There is a penalty for withdrawal before age 59 $\frac{1}{2}$, which is apparently intended to discourage the use of IRAs for nonretirement saving.

Whether IRAs are an important form of saving for retirement depends on how much is contributed. Whether they serve as a substitute for private pension plans depends on who contributes. The short-run tax cost of IRAs also depends on how much is contributed and on the marginal tax rates of contributors, since contributions are not taxed. Possibly the most important question, however, is the relationship between IRA contributions and other forms of saving. What is the net

David A. Wise is the John F. Stambaugh Professor of Political Economy at the John F. Kennedy School of Government, Harvard University, and a research associate of the National Bureau of Economic Research.

3

effect of IRA accounts on individual saving? That is the primary focus of this paper.

Two central questions arise in considering the effect of newly available IRAs on net saving. The first is the extent to which IRA contributions are made with funds withdrawn from other saving accounts. Presumably such substitution would be made by taking funds from existing liquid asset balances, such as other saving accounts. A second question is whether new saving would have been placed in other accounts were it not for the availability of IRAs. Would the new saving have been made anyway?

This paper is based primarily on my work with Steven Venti, with some comparisons drawn from my analysis of Canadian Registered Retirement Saving Plans (RRSP).

1.1   The Incentive Effects of IRAs

Two characteristics of IRAs provide an incentive to increase saving. First, it costs less in terms of current consumption to save through an IRA. To save $1,000 in a regular saving account requires that $1,000 less be spent for current goods and services. But for a person in the 30% marginal tax bracket, for example, $1,000 can be saved by reducing expenditure for current goods and services by only $700, $1,000 less the $300 in tax that does not have to be paid on the $1,000 IRA contribution.

Second, while tax must be paid on the interest that accrues in a regular saving account, the interest that accrues in an IRA is not taxed. Suppose, for example, that the interest rate is 10%, the marginal tax rate is 30%, and that a dollar saved at age twenty-five is not withdrawn until age sixty-five. Assume also that the marginal tax rate when the dollar is saved is the same as the marginal tax rate when it is withdrawn. Then at age sixty-five the accumulated value of the IRA contribution after taxes would be 3.32 times the value of a contribution to a conventional saving account. It would be worth 1.82 times the value of a conventional saving account if the dollar were saved at age forty-five. The IRA advantage increases with the interest rate, the marginal tax rate, and the number of years that the money is left in the account. If $2,000 were placed in an IRA account each year beginning at age twenty-five, the after-tax value of the account by age sixty-five would be $789,000; placed in a regular saving account, the value would be only $320,000. Again, the IRA advantage increases with the interest rate, the marginal tax rate, and the number of years over which contributions are made.

On the other hand, once money is placed in an IRA account, there is a 10% penalty for withdrawal before age 59½. In this sense, the IRA is less liquid than a regular savings account. Of course some persons may consider this an advantage; it may help to ensure behavior that would not otherwise be the case by being a means of self-control. However, if the funds are to be withdrawn before age 59½, whether it would be better to save the money in an IRA or a regular account depends on the interest rate, the marginal tax rate, and the length of time that the money will remain in the account. At an interest rate of 10% and a marginal tax rate of 30%, funds would have to be left in an IRA for 5.6 years to break even. At an interest rate of 2% and a marginal tax rate of 30%, the funds would have to be left for 26.1 years. At an interest rate of 10% and a marginal tax rate of 50%, they would have to be left for 4.8 years. The number years to break even is lower with higher interest rates and with higher marginal tax rates. Thus, the incentive to save through IRAs because of their higher return should be greater for persons in higher tax brackets, and the disincentive because they are less liquid should be less as the tax bracket is higher.

There is an additional reason why total saving might be less with the availability of IRAs. Because of the greater return on IRA contributions, the amount of saving necessary to achieve a given level of retirement savings is less if the saving is done through IRAs. For example, again at an interest rate of 10% and a marginal tax rate of 30%, to achieve $1 million in retirement saving by age sixty-five would require giving up $4,377 per year in expenditures for current goods and services beginning at age twenty-five if saving were through a regular account, but only $1,775 if the saving were through an IRA. Thus, to attain the same level of consumption after retirement, one need forgo less consumption before retirement if saving is done through IRAs. This is what has led some to argue that there could in principle be less saving with than without IRA accounts.

Finally, the promotion of IRAs may have a substantial effect on their use. They are advertised widely and are available through almost any bank and through many other financial institutions. Their promotion has typically emphasized the avoidance of current taxes through IRA contributions, as well as the importance of prudent planning for future retirement. Of course, the ultimate effect of IRAs on saving is the net result of all these factors.

To put the subsequent discussion of findings on that issue in perspective, it is useful first to consider summary data on IRA contributions and on other forms of saving.

1.2 Descriptive Data

Sixteen percent of families with wage earners had IRAs, according to the recently released 1983 Survey of Consumer Finances (SCF).

Although the likelihood of contributing to an IRA is much greater for high- than for low-income families, almost 70% of contributors have incomes less than $50,000, as shown in table 1.1. Almost no families with incomes under $10,000 have them, and only about 7% of families with incomes between $10,000 and $20,000 do. Slightly more than half of those with incomes above $50,000 contribute to IRAs, based on the SCF. In addition, older persons are considerably more likely than younger ones to contribute. Yet because there are many fewer high-income than middle-income families, the preponderance of contributors is at the middle-income levels.

The results of the formal analysis discussed here rely in part on the relationship between 1982 IRA contributions on the one hand and on changes in "overall savings and reserve funds" on the other. Only 32% of respondents to the SCF survey reported an overall increase in savings and reserve funds in 1982. But those who made IRA contributions were much more likely than noncontributors to report an increase. Table 1.2 shows the proportion with an increase (by income interval)

Table 1.1   IRA Contribution by Income

Income Interval ($ Thousands)	% with IRAs	% of Contributors
0– 10	1	2
10– 20	7	15
20– 30	14	17
30– 40	25	20
40– 50	34	15
50–100	51	24
100 +	65	8
All	16	100

Table 1.2   Increase in Savings and Reserve Funds by Income and by IRA Contribution Status

Income Interval ($ Thousands)	% with an Increase in Savings and Reserve Funds	(% of IRA Contributors with an Increase) ÷ (% of Noncontributors with an Increase)
0– 10	14	...
10– 20	26	1.54
20– 30	35	1.77
30– 40	44	1.68
40– 50	50	1.47
50–100	56	1.40
100 +	54	2.19
All	32	2.10

and the proportion of IRA contributors versus noncontributors with an increase.

Suppose that IRA contributions were typically taken from savings and reserve fund balances. If savings and reserve funds include IRAs, there would be no change in overall savings and reserve funds. If the latter were interpreted to exclude IRAs, contributions to IRAs would be associated with a decline in savings and reserve funds. Apparently neither is true. Persons who contribute to IRAs are much more likely to indicate an increase than those who do not. Overall, contributors are more than twice as likely as noncontributors to indicate an increase, although this number in part reflects different distributions of contributors and noncontributors by income and age. The average of the ratios over groups defined by income and age is 1.77 (see Venti and Wise 1987). Thus, these numbers suggest that there are savers and nonsavers and that savers contribute both to IRAs and to other savings instruments; the positive relationship reflects an "individual-specific" saving effect.

To put the level of IRA contributions in perspective and to help to interpret the analysis here, it is useful to know the magnitude of individual wealth holdings. The median wealth of families in the sample is $22,900, excluding pensions and Social Security wealth (as shown in table 1.3).[1] Most of this wealth is nonliquid, the preponderance of it being housing. Consistent with other evidence, a large proportion of individuals have very little wealth other than housing; they save very

Table 1.3   **Assets by Type and by Income ($ Thousands)**

Income Intervals	Total Wealth	Nonliquid Assets	All Financial Assets	Financial Assets Excluding Stocks and Bonds
0– 10	.5	.07	.1	.1
10– 20	10.0	.1	.7	.7
20– 30	28.3	24.5	1.9	1.7
30– 40	50.5	44.2	4.0	3.5
40– 50	80.6	64.9	8.5	5.5
50–100	123.6	92.5	20.0	12.8
100 +	279.0	197.5	38.0	30.4
All	22.9	18.7	1.3	1.2

1. The following breakdown of wealth is used throughout this paper: liquid assets: checking accounts, certificates of deposit, savings accounts, money market accounts, savings bonds; other financial assets: stocks, bonds, trusts; IRAs and Keoghs: balances; other assets: value of home, other property, receivables; debt: mortgage and consumer debt. Total wealth is the sum of the first four categories minus debt. Wealth does *not* include the cash value of life insurance, the value of motor vehicles, and pension and social security wealth.

little. The median for all families is $1,200. For families earning $30,000–$40,000 with a head forty-five to fifty-four years old, the median is only $4,600. While most people have some liquid assets, only about 20% have financial assets in the form of stocks or bonds. Therefore, it is clear that most people have not been accumulating financial assets at a rate close to the $2,000 per year that an IRA allows.

While IRA contributors have larger holdings of financial assets than noncontributors, even their holdings are much lower than the assets that would have been accumulated had their annual savings equaled the typical IRA contribution. The average IRA contribution (of SCF families who contributed) was about $2,500. (There were two wage earners in many contributing families.) The median of family liquid asset holdings among IRA contributors by income interval is shown in table 1.4. Recall that almost 70% of contributors have family incomes of less than $50,000.[2] It is clear that these families typically have not been saving close to $2,500 per year in financial assets. Thus 1982 IRA contributions seem large relative to apparent past saving. As would be expected, and as was demonstrated by the relationship between IRA contributions and changes in savings and reserve funds, IRA contributors tend to be savers. Not only do they make IRA contributions, but they are also more likely to report an increase in overall savings and reserve funds; and, because they are savers, they have accumulated more assets.

It is sometimes implied that, because many IRA contributors have previously accumulated other savings and could have funded IRA contributions by withdrawals from these balances, they did in fact do that. But our data provide no evidence of that. Even responses to survey questions that ask where the funds for IRA contributions came from are difficult to interpret. Since most people do not carry $2,000 in cash,

Table 1.4   Financial Assets of IRA Contributors ($ Thousands)

Income Interval	Financial Assets Excluding Stocks and Bonds
0– 10	2.46
10– 20	3.10
20– 30	4.00
30– 40	7.10
40– 50	8.75
50–100	16.10
100+	35.00
All	8.51

2. Fifty percent of contributors have less than $8,510 in liquid assets; 25% have less than $3,000.

when asked where the money for an IRA contribution came from, they often respond that it came from another saving account. But the fact that the money was taken from another account does not suggest that there was no new saving. Rather, the issue is what would have happened to the money had it not been used to make the IRA contribution. Would the money have stayed in the alternative saving account, or would it have been used for some other purpose, such as the purchase of new furniture? Our data make it clear that families are not likely to accumulate financial assets, and thus it would appear that $2,000 removed from a saving account to put into an IRA would not typically have remained in the alternative saving account for long; at least financial assets would not have accumulated at the rate of $2,000 per year.

According to IRS data, total IRA contributions in 1982 were about $28.3 billion and there were about 12 million contributors; 1983 contributions totaled $32.1 billion, with 13.6 million contributors; and, in 1984, there were $35.8 billion in contributions and 15.4 million contributors (see U.S. Internal Revenue Service 1985, 1986). The extent to which the same people contributed each year is not reported. However, evidence based on Canadian data suggests that the same people tend to contribute year after year to the Canadian equivalent of the IRA. Thus the rapidly expanding balances in these accounts, together with low prior balances on financial assets, may suggest more saving with IRAs than would have occurred in their absence.

Although detailed data are not available, anecdotal evidence suggests that many IRA contributions are made just before tax-filing time. Last-minute contributors apparently do not want to commit funds for long-term saving before they have considered their financial situation at the end of the year. They apparently do not have such funds already committed in another account; if they did, it would pay to transfer the funds at the beginning rather than the end of the year. Thus, to the extent that last-minute contributions are made, they suggest that contributors are liquidity constrained and do not consider other funds to be readily available for this purpose.

These descriptive data, although suggestive, do not allow direct estimates of the net savings effect of IRAs. The analysis summarized here is directed to that end.

1.3 The Results of Statistical Estimation

Much of the evidence reported here is based on analysis of the 1983 SCF (see Venti and Wise 1986, 1987). It is compared with results based on the Special Supplement to the May 1983 Current Population Survey (CPS) (see Venti and Wise 1985) and with results of analysis of comparable Canadian Registered Retirement Saving Plan (RRSP) (see Wise

1984, 1985) data. While the CPS and the Canadian data allow analysis of determinants of IRA and RRSP contributions, only the SCF allows joint analysis of IRA contributions with changes in other saving. This is necessary to determine the net effect of IRAs. The formal model analyzes IRA contributions jointly with changes in other savings and reserve funds, taking account of the limit on IRA contributions. In particular, the analysis considers non-IRA saving by persons who do not have IRAs or who have not contributed up to the IRA limit, compared with the non-IRA saving of persons who have reached the IRA limit. First I shall discuss evidence on the determinants of IRA contributions themselves, and then I will consider the effects of IRAs on net saving.

1.3.1   The Determinants of IRA Contributions

Income is the most important determinant of IRA contributions. Holding income constant, contributions also tend to increase with age. Further, there is a strong relationship between education and IRA contributions. Indeed, a year of education is equal to more than two years of age and more than $30,000 of liquid wealth in term of IRA contributions. This is consistent with other evidence of a wide variation in saving behavior among segments of the population. It is of course also consistent with the emphasis on savers versus nonsavers; some individuals tend to save and do so in several forms, while others tend not to save.

In addition, the estimates show that persons without private pension plans are no more likely than persons with them to contribute to an IRA, controlling for other individual attributes such as income. Furthermore, persons with private pension plans save more in non-IRA forms. On the other hand, the evidence shows that, while persons without private pension plans save less in all forms jointly, they devote a larger proportion of what they do save to IRAs. It would appear, however, that the legislative goal of disproportionately increasing the retirement saving of persons without private pension plans is not being realized.

Finally, while the incentive effects of IRAs described at the beginning of the paper suggested that persons in higher tax brackets would be more likely than those in lower tax brackets to contribute to IRAs, we have not been able to demonstrate convincingly an increasing preference for IRAs with increasing marginal tax rates. The estimated effect of income versus the tax rate is very sensitive to the model used for estimation. This finding, in conjunction with a very strong preference for IRAs as opposed to other forms of savings, leads me to believe that the widespread promotion of IRAs may be the most important reason for increased saving.

Because the Canadian and American tax-deferred accounts are very similar in their general outlines, it is informative to compare the relationship between personal attributes and contributions to the plans in the two countries. The Canadian counterpart to the U.S. IRA and Keogh plans is the RRSP. While the RRSP contribution limits are considerably higher than the IRA limits, the estimated relationships between income and other personal attributes on the one hand and the amount that individuals would like to contribute to the plans on the other are very close in the two countries (see Wise 1985 and Venti and Wise 1985). This suggests that saving behavior in the two countries is very similar in this respect.

The Canadian RRSP has been in effect since 1956, but was substantially expanded in the early 1970s. The personal saving rate has been much higher in Canada than in the United States since the Canadian program was expanded. Evidence reported here suggests that personal savings in the United States would be considerably higher if the IRA limit were raised. The Canadian RRSP limits will be raised, very substantially for some persons, beginning in 1986.

1.3.2 IRA versus Other Saving

Estimates based on the relationship between IRA contributions and changes in other saving balances show that individuals typically are much more inclined to save through IRAs than through other forms of saving. For example, the results suggest that, averaged over all persons in the sample, with no IRA limit, possibly three to five cents of the last dollar of income would be allocated to other financial assets saving, while as much as fifteen cents would be allocated to IRA saving. This result is consistent with the very low level of personal saving in the United States in recent years, other than in the form of housing. It suggests that saving should be larger with than without the possibility of IRAs.

After controlling for income, age, and other personal attributes, estimates show that persons who are likely to make IRA contributions are also more likely to save in other forms. This is consistent with the summary data presented earlier. The results also show that total wealth is in fact negatively related to IRA saving as well as to saving in other financial asset forms. Distinction of liquid from nonliquid wealth shows that nonliquid assets are negatively related to both IRA and other forms of financial saving. Liquid assets, which are likely to be the most readily transferable to IRA accounts, are positively related to IRA contributions, but they are also positively related to other financial assets saving. Indeed, the relationship to other saving is much greater than the relationship to IRA saving. For example, a $1,000 increase in accumulated liquid assets is associated with a $45 increase in other financial asset saving but only a $5 increase in IRA saving. These results are all consistent with differences in saving behavior among individuals. Persons who have accumulated financial assets in the past are likely to continue to accumulate them in non-IRA forms and are also likely to accumulate financial assets in the form of IRAs. On the other hand, persons who have accumulated large nonliquid asset balances, primarily in the form of housing, are less likely either to contribute to IRAs or to save through other liquid financial asset forms, controlling for other variables such as income and age. This evidence provides little support for the possibility that IRA contributions were typically funded by withdrawals that would not otherwise have been made from other liquid asset balances.

1.3.3   Simulations of the Effect of IRA Limit Changes

To demonstrate the estimated effect of IRAs on net saving, Steven Venti and I simulated the effect of increases in the IRA limit on IRA saving itself and on other saving. We have also simulated the effects of several recently proposed limit changes. The first, which we call the Treasury Plan, would increase the limit for an employed person from $2,000 to $2,500 and for a nonworking spouse from $250 to $2,500. Thus, the contribution limit for a husband and nonworking wife would increase from $2,250 to $5,000. A Modified Treasury Plan increases the limit for an employed person from $2,000 to $2,500, but it only increases the limit for a nonworking spouse to $500 from $250. Finally, the President's Plan would leave the limit for an employed person at $2,000 but would raise the limit for a nonworking spouse from $250 to $2,000. For comparison, we also simulate savings under the current limit.

The predicted changes may be interpreted as changes in saving if the IRA limit had been higher in 1982. It is important to remember that non-IRA saving undoubtedly excludes changes in nonliquid wealth, such as housing. For example, the possible substitution between IRAs and housing wealth in the long run would not be reflected in these estimates. They are intended, however, to indicate the extent to which IRA contributions in 1982 were simply a substitute for forms of saving other than nonliquid assets. The results are shown in table 1.5. The top portion pertains to individuals who are at the IRA limit, since only this group would be affected by an increase in the limit. The bottom shows simulated contributions for all families.

These estimates suggest that the Treasury Plan would increase average IRA saving by $1,091 for families who are at the current limit. Only 20% of the IRA increase is offset by a reduction in other financial assets. Possibly the best indicator of saving is change in consumption. The average change in "consumption" (as defined implicitly in this

Table 1.5   **Simulated Effects of Changes in IRA Limits**

	Base		Change		Change		Change	
	Current Plan (2,000/250)		Treasury Plan (2,500/2,500)		Mod. Treas. Plan (2,500/500)		President's Plan (2,000/ 2,000)	
	IRA	Other	IRA	Other	IRA	Other	IRA	Other
Families at the IRA limit:								
Avg. contribution	3,069	3,831	1,091	−210	754	−143	351	−67
% change	—	—	+36	−5	+25	−4	+11	−2
All families:								
Avg. contribution	522	111	143	−28	99	−19	46	−9
% change	—	—	+27	−25	+19	−17	+9	−8

Table 1.6   **Source of IRA Funds, by Plan**

	Treasury Plan (2,500/2,500)		Mod. Treasury Plan (2,500/500)		President's Plan (2,000/2,000)	
	Amount	%	Amount	%	Amount	%
Families at the IRA limit						
Change in IRA saving	1,091	100.0	754	100.0	351	100.0
Change in other saving	−210	19.2	−143	19.0	−67	19.1
Change in consumption	−493	45.2	−344	45.6	−162	46.2
Change in taxes	−388	35.6	−267	35.4	−122	34.8
All families						
Change in IRA saving	143	100.0	99	100.0	46	100.0
Change in other saving	−28	19.6	−19	19.2	−9	19.6
Change in consumption	−65	45.5	−45	45.5	−21	45.7
Change in taxes	−50	35.0	−35	35.4	−16	34.8

analysis) under each plan is shown in table 1.6, together with changes in other saving and taxes. For example, about 45% of the $1,091 IRA increase under the Treasury Plan is funded by reduced consumption, according to these measures, and about 35% by reduced taxes, with approximately 20% coming from reduction in other saving. These estimates are based on one version of the analysis that shows somewhat larger reductions in other savings than are predicted with other specifications of the model.

Under the Treasury Plan, for example, average IRA contributions would be $665 ($522 plus the $143 increase due to the higher limit). This level of contribution could not, of course, be sustained long by funding from median liquid asset balances of $1,200, as reported in the summary tables above. The average contribution of all contributors would be $3,135; this level could not be sustained for long from the median liquid asset balance of contributors of $8,510.

I believe that the estimated IRA increases are relatively accurate. Estimates based on May 1983 CPS data, which differ in several respects from the SCF data, show virtually the same effects of limit increases on IRA contributions (see Venti and Wise, 1985). For example, the simulated increase under the Treasury Plan for all families is 27% based on the SCF data versus 30% based on the CPS data. While it is not possible with U.S. data to test the accuracy of the predictions directly, it is possible to do so for Canadian RRSPs. This is a useful comparison because, as mentioned above, the estimated behavior of Canadians with respect to RRSPs is very similar to the estimated behavior of Americans with respect to IRAs. In Canada, however, RRSPs have been in existence for some time and the limits have changed substantially. In particular, even when the nominal limits has remained the same, it has changed a great deal in real terms because of inflation. Because data are available over time, it is possible to use estimates in one year to predict for a later year or to use estimates in a later year to extrapolate for an earlier year. In Canada, this exercise yields predictions that are very close to actual RRSP contributions (see Wise 1984, 1985).

1.4 Conclusions

Increasing the IRA limits would lead to substantial increases in tax-deferred saving, according to evidence based on the 1983 Survey of Consumer Finances. For example, the recent Treasury Plan would increase IRA contributions by about 30%. Virtually the same estimate was obtained in a previous analysis based on CPS data, suggesting that this conclusion may be relatively robust. The primary focus of this paper, however, has been the effect of limit increases on other saving. How much of the IRA increase would be offset by reduction in non-tax-deferred saving? The weight of the evidence suggests that only a small proportion of the increase would be offset by reductions in other financial assets, possibly 20% or less. Our estimates suggest that approximately 45%–55% of the IRA increase would be funded by reduction in consumption and about 35% by reduced taxes. While it is difficult to demonstrate, the widespread promotion of IRAs may be the most important reason for increased saving through them.

The model fits the data well and, in particular, accurately distinguishes the savings decisions of persons at the IRA limit versus the decisions of those who are not. The greatest potential uncertainty about the results and the greatest statistical complication for analysis stem from the limited information on non-IRA saving and the associated difficulty of obtaining direct estimates of the degree of substitution between tax-deferred and non-tax-deferred saving. I have addressed these issues by considering the sensitivity of our conclusions to specification changes, including assumptions about the interpretation of key variables and the extent of substitution underlying observed outcomes for saving. Although the magnitude of the estimated reduction in other saving with increases in the IRA limit is sensitive to specification changes, the reduction as a percentage of the IRA increase is invariably small.

In addition to these primary conclusions, the evidence suggests substantial variation in saving behavior among segments of the population. We also find that IRAs do not serve as a substitute for private pension plans, although persons without private plans devote a larger proportion of their lower total saving to IRAs. Thus, the legislative goal of disproportionately increasing retirement saving among persons without pension plans is apparently not being realized. But the more general goal of increasing individual saving is.

References

U.S. Internal Revenue Service. 1985. *SOI Bulletin* 4, no. 3 (Winter 1984–85).
———. 1986. *SOI Bulletin* 5, n. 3 (Winter 1985–86).
Venti, Steven F., and David A., Wise. 1985. The determinants of IRA contributions and the effect of limit changes. NBER Working Paper 1731. In *Pensions in the U.S. economy*, ed. Zvi Bodie, John Shoven, and David A. Wise. Chicago: University of Chicago Press: In press.
———. 1986. Tax-deferred accounts, constrained choice, and estimation of individual saving. *Review of Economic Studies* 53 (August): 579–601.
———. 1987. IRAs and saving. NBER Working Paper 1879. In *The effects of taxation on capital accumulation*, ed. Martin Feldstein. Chicago: University of Chicago Press.
Wise, David A. 1984. The effects of policy changes on RRSP contributions. Prepared for the Tax Policy and Legislation Branch of the Canadian Department of Finance (March 1984).
———. 1985. Contributors and contributions to Registered Retirement Savings Plans. Prepared for the Tax Policy and Legislation Branch of the Canadian Department of Finance (April 1985).

2   Rates, Realizations, and Revenues of Capital Gains

Lawrence B. Lindsey

The effect of the capital gains tax on the sale of capital assets and the realization of gains on these assets has been a matter of substantial academic and political controversy. Capital gains are only taxed when an asset is sold, so inclusion of gains in taxable income is largely discretionary from the point of view of the taxpayer. As a result, sensitivity to tax rates is probably greater for capital gains income than for other kinds of income.

This sensitivity may take a number of forms. Capital gains and losses on assets held for less than a specified time period, currently six months, are taxed as ordinary income, while gains and losses on assets held for longer periods of time are taxed at lower rates. Planning of sales around this capital gains holding period was studied by Kaplan (1981), who concluded that eliminating the distinction between long-term and short-term gains and taxing all assets under current long-term rules would enhance capital gains tax revenue. Fredland, Gray, and Sunley (1968) also found that the length of the holding period had a significant effect on the timing of asset sales.

The deferral of taxes on capital gains until realization enhances the incentive to postpone selling assets. A taxpayer might defer selling one asset and purchasing another with a higher pretax return because capital gains tax on the sale makes the transaction unprofitable. This is known as the "lock-in" effect. Feldstein, Slemrod, and Yitzhaki (1980) estimated that the effect of lock-in was substantial enough to imply that a reduction in tax rates from their 1978 levels would increase tax revenue. Their study focused on sales of common stock using 1973 tax return

Lawrence B. Lindsey is an assistant professor of economics at Harvard University and a faculty research fellow of the National Bureau of Economic Research.

data. The results mirrored those of an earlier work by Feldstein and Yitzhaki (1977), which relies on data from the 1963–64 Federal Reserve Board Survey of the Financial Characteristics of Consumers.

Brannon (1974) found evidence of reduced realizations of capital gains as a result of tax rate increases in 1970 and 1971. A lock-in effect was also identified by Auten (1979). Later work by Auten and Clotfelter (1979) found a substantially greater sensitivity of capital gains realizations to short-term fluctuations in the tax rate than to long-term, average tax rate levels. Minarik (1981) studied the lock-in effect and concluded that a 1% reduction in the capital gains tax rate would raise realizations, but by substantially less than 1%. The U.S. Department of the Treasury (1985) released a report to the Congress that presented substantially higher estimates of the elasticity of capital gains realizations to tax rates and concluded that the tax rate reductions of 1978 had the effect of increasing capital gains tax revenue.

The objective of the present paper is to examine the relationship among capital gains tax rates, the level of realizations of long-term gains subject to tax, and revenues from capital gains taxation over an extended period of time. The Tax Reform Act of 1969 began an era of high variability in the capital gains tax rate, which had been relatively constant for the preceding fifteen years. Further changes in the tax reform bills of 1976, 1978, and 1981 continued this variability. Smaller changes in the capital gains tax rate occurred in intervening years due to changes in ordinary tax rates, changes in other provisions of the tax law, and bracket creep.

The changes in the effective capital gains tax rate that resulted from these laws were quite complex and often involved the interaction of several provisions. This paper estimates the effective marginal tax rate on capital gains for various income groups over the period 1965–82. The tax rate calculations use the detailed tabulation data of personal income tax returns provided by the *Statistics of Income*. These calculations show smaller actual variability in rates than suggested by other studies that relied on calculations of maximum effective tax rates.

Sector balance sheets and reconciliation statements from the Federal Reserve Board's *Flow of Funds* series are used to estimate the level and composition of the wealth of the household sector. This data also provide estimates of the change in the value of these holdings caused by movements in asset prices. These changes are closely related to the stock of unrealized capital gains in the household sector, which is the base from which capital gains are realized and reported on tax returns.

2.1 Measuring Capital Gains Tax Rates

The Internal Revenue Code of 1954 distinguished between gains on assets held at least six months and those held longer. The former were taxed as ordinary income, while the latter, termed long-term gains, were given a 50% exclusion from taxable income. However, this exclusion was limited to net capital gains: long-term gains in excess of short-term losses. Therefore, to the extent that long-term gains simply canceled short-term losses, the long-term marginal tax rate equaled the short-term rate, which was the same as the tax rate on ordinary income.

Poterba (1985) examined 1982 tax return data and found that taxpayers with net long-term gains composed the majority of all returns reporting capital gains or losses. He noted, however, that a sizable fraction of taxpayers were subject to the capital loss limitation and therefore could realize additional long-term gains without incurring any additional current tax liability. These taxpayers are unaffected by the current marginal tax rate on capital gains, generate no capital gains tax liability, and are therefore neglected in the present study.

This study focuses only on taxpayers with long-term gains in excess of short-term losses. Inclusion of taxpayers with net capital losses would imply a lower level of capital gains revenue and a lower revenue-maximizing capital gains tax rate than is reported here. The current rule is that the tax rate on these net long-term gains is 40% of a taxpayer's ordinary rate. Since ordinary rates currently go up to 50%, the top marginal tax rate on long-term gains is 20%.

Prior to 1982, the top tax rate on capital gains was always higher than this. Ordinary tax rates ranged up to 70% in earlier years. Prior to November 1978, half of all capital gains were subject to tax, not the current 40%. In addition, there were a number of other provisions of the tax code that affected the capital gains tax rate. These included the Alternative Tax Computation, the Additional Minimum Tax, the Maximum Tax on Personal Service Income, and the Alternative Minimum Tax. The effect of each was calculated using detailed tabulation from the *Statistics of Income.*

The Alternative Tax Computation permitted taxpayers to limit the marginal tax rate on at least some of their capital gains to 25%. Although this provision is generally described as having "effectively truncated the tax rate schedule,"[1] careful analysis of the data suggests that this was not the case.

Prior to 1970, taxpayers could calculate their tax using the ordinary tax schedule to compute the tax on their non-capital-gains income and adding 50% of their taxable capital gains to figure their total tax. Taxpayers could pay either this "alternative" amount or the tax they would owe using the ordinary tax consumption. However, because of the way the tax was designed, a significant fraction of high-income capital gains

---

1. See, e.g., the U.S. Department of Treasury's report to the Congress on the capital gains tax reductions of 1978, p. 35. A similar statement appears in the description of the alternative tax computation in the *Statistics of Income 1966:* "The effect of this computation was a maximum tax of 25 percent on net long-term capital gain" (p. 164).

taxpayers did not choose the alternative tax but paid the ordinary tax: it involved a higher marginal tax rate but a lower average tax rate on their capital gains income. For example, in 1966, one-sixth of all capital gains taxpayers with adjusted gross income (AGI) between $200,000 and $500,000 paid the ordinary tax, as did one-quarter with AGI between $100,000 and $200,000.[2]

Consider the taxpayer with long-term gains of $200,000, other income of $50,000, and exclusions and itemized deductions of $40,000. The taxpayer excludes half of the long-term gain from taxable income, leaving an AGI of $150,000 and a taxable income of $110,000. Using the tax schedule of the era (1965–69), the ordinary tax computation would produce a tax liability of $51,380, but the alternative tax computation involved a tax of $51,820.

This taxpayer would elect to be taxed under the ordinary schedule because it produced a lower tax liability. However, the marginal tax rate on capital gains under the ordinary method is 31% compared with the 25% under the alternative method. Due to the design of the tax, the alternative method could produce a higher *average* tax rate even though it produced a lower *marginal* tax rate.

The Tax Reform Act of 1969 changed the alternative tax computation by limiting the lower marginal rate to the first $50,000 of net long-term capital gains. As a result of this change, less than half of high-income taxpayers had a low marginal tax rate on capital gains because of the alternative tax computation. In spite of the ineffectiveness of this provision at the margin, a substantial amount of tax revenue was lost by extending the inframarginal benefit to these taxpayers. The net results were a low tax rate on capital gains that the taxpayer was going to realize anyway and a high tax rate on capital gains about which the taxpayer was undecided. This produced the wrong type of incentive system for generating capital gains tax revenue.

The Additional Minimum Tax was levied in two forms, one from 1970 through 1975 and one from 1976 through 1978. Both had the peculiar feature of lowering the additional tax rate as the taxpayer's taxable income rose. Under the Additional Minimum Tax, a taxpayer summed a list of tax preference items that included the excluded portion of capital gains and paid a tax on the excess of this amount over a base. In the early version of the tax, this base was the sum of $30,000 plus the taxpayer's ordinary tax liability. Later, this base was lowered to the greater of $10,000 or one-half of the taxpayer's ordinary tax liability.

In either event, as the taxpayer's ordinary taxes rose, this base amount, termed an "offset," also increased. When a taxpayer realized an additional dollar of capital gains, the excluded fifty cents entered

2. These data were derived from the *Statistics of Income 1966*, p. 94.

the minimum tax as a preference, while the rest was taxed at ordinary tax rates, thus also increasing the offset. At a capital gains tax rate of 25%, half of the preference was offset. At a rate of 35%, thirty-five cents of the fifty-cent capital gains preference was offset. So, at high ordinary tax rates, the amount subject to the minimum tax was lower, and the additional minimum tax rate was correspondingly lower.

The changes in 1976 not only reduced the tax base but also increased the additional tax rate from 10% to 15%. The IRS estimates that this resulted in an elevenfold increase in the number of taxpayers paying the minimum tax and a sixfold increase in minimum tax revenues.[3]

The Maximum Tax on Personal Service Income, enacted as part of the Tax Reform Act of 1969, lowered the tax rate on wage, salary, and professional income below that on other types of income for many taxpayers. Instead of the statutory 70% top rate, the tax rate on personal service income was taxed at 60% in 1971 and 50% thereafter. As Lindsey (1981) showed, the maximum tax was ineffective at achieving this lower rate for the vast majority of high-income taxpayers. However, a complex interaction between the maximum tax and capital gains had the effect of raising the capital gains tax rate for many taxpayers.

Every dollar of capital gains income converted a dollar of earned income, taxed at the low rate, into "unearned" income, taxed at the higher rate. This had the effect of adding as much as ten percentage points to the effective capital gains tax rate. The conversion of earned into unearned income due to capital gains became known as "poisoning."

Changes in the rules on poisoning in 1976 dramatically increased the effect of this provision. For example, the effect on the capital gains tax rate for taxpayers in the $100,000–$200,000 income group rose sixfold between 1976 and 1977. This led to a dramatic upward shift in the capital gains tax rate until poisoning was eliminated in 1979.

The Alternative Minimum Tax replaced the Additional Minimum Tax on capital gains beginning in 1979. This tax was levied at 10%, 20%, or 25% on a tax base that was broader than the ordinary tax base. The taxpayer had to pay the greater of his ordinary tax or his alternative minimum tax. Since these tax rates were generally lower than the ordinary tax rates on capital gains, the alternative minimum tax lowered the effective tax rate on capital gains.

Table 2.1 presents calculations of the average effective tax rate on capital gains faced by taxpayers with net long-term capital gains. The calculations weighted all taxpayers with net gains equally in order to minimize the statistical simultaneity between the tax rate and the level of realizations. The tax rates in table 2.1 reflect the effects of each of

3. These data were presented in *Statistics of Income 1976*, table 3B, p. 83.

Table 2.1   Average Effective Marginal Tax Rate on Capital Gains

	Income Class					
Year	Under $50,000	$50,000– $100,000	$100,000– $200,000	$200,000– $500,000	$500,000– $1,000,000	Over $1,000,000
1965	11.1	25.5	26.5	26.6	26.0	25.3
1966	11.1	25.5	26.5	26.6	26.0	25.3
1967	12.5	25.5	26.5	26.6	26.0	25.3
1968	13.4	27.4	28.4	28.5	27.9	27.1
1969	13.8	28.0	29.0	29.1	28.5	27.7
1970	12.9	27.8	30.5	32.2	32.1	32.0
1971	12.5	26.3	29.1	32.0	33.3	33.9
1972	12.5	26.6	28.7	32.5	33.9	34.6
1973	12.5	26.6	28.9	32.8	34.3	35.0
1974	12.0	26.3	28.9	32.6	33.6	34.4
1975	11.6	26.3	28.8	32.5	33.5	34.7
1976	11.5	27.2	29.9	34.0	36.1	37.3
1977	10.8	27.8	31.7	36.3	39.2	41.2
1978	10.6	27.8	32.2	36.3	37.9	39.1
1979	10.6	19.4	25.3	27.3	27.0	26.9
1980	10.6	19.5	25.4	27.6	27.6	27.6
1981	10.8	19.1	22.9	24.1	24.2	24.2
1982	11.2	17.6	20.0	20.0	20.0	20.0

the provisions discussed here and other changes in the tax law that occurred during this period.

2.2 The Value of Personal Assets

Evaluation of the importance of capital gains tax rates in determining the level of realizations is complicated by changes in the value of personal wealth including accrued but unrealized gains. The Federal Reserve Board issues a quarterly *Flow of Funds* report on the holdings of various sectors of the U.S. economy, including the household sector, which is the focus of this study.

The components of household wealth include many elements such as cash, checking and saving deposits, and pension fund and insurance wealth on which taxpayers do not realize capital gains. This study therefore grouped household wealth into nontraded assets such as these and tradeable assets on which taxable capital gains are reported and taxed.

Tradeable assets include land, residential structures, corporate equities, and equity in noncorporate businesses. This last category includes the value of nonresidential real estate held by households. Tangible assets, such as consumer durables, that are seldom traded were excluded. These tradeable assets constituted about two-thirds of household wealth over the period of the study. They also accounted for some 97% of the value of capital gains reported on tax returns.[4]

The components of this tradeable wealth varied over time. For example, nonresidential real estate peaked at 39.4% at the beginning of the period. Corporate equities fell from nearly 23% of total wealth in 1968 to only 9.5% in 1979.

In order to model this variation, household wealth was apportioned among six income groups on a component-by-component basis. Each component of wealth was allocated according to the distribution of income likely to flow from it, as reported on tax returns. For example, the distribution of corporate equities in a given year was assumed to be the same as the distribution of dividends reported in that year.

Shares of wealth were therefore determined from the same tax-based data as the distribution of reported capital gains. Observations on individual income classes in each year were therefore independent of observations in other years. At the same time, the aggregate level of wealth was determined independently of the data on capital gains realizations.

The *Flow of Funds* data also include sectoral reconciliation statements that estimate the change in asset prices. These revaluations were computed for periods ranging from one to seven years. They were converted into inflation-adjusted terms to reflect the real value of asset appreciation for each year studied. However, the data suggested that revaluation periods of more than one year did not significantly affect the rate of realizations. Rather, accrued capital gains over long periods became indistinguishable from other types of wealth.

2.3 Econometric Results

The data on capital gains tax rates, realizations, and household wealth were analyzed statistically. The basic results showed that a one-percentage-point reduction in the capital gains tax rate resulted in 6.2% more net gains realized. The implication of this finding is that revenues from capital gains taxes are maximized when the capital gains tax rate is 16%. At higher tax rates, the revenue gained from taxing realized gains at higher rates is more than offset by a reduction in the amount of capital gains realized. At lower tax rates, the revenue lost from the lower rate is not recouped by the broadening of the tax base. This estimate of the revenue-maximizing rate is best interpreted as being in the center of a range of possible rates from 14.3% to 18.5%.

Capital gains realizations also appeared to rise in direct proportion to the value of traded assets in household wealth. This is as expected.

---

4. This was calculated from U.S. Department of Treasury's (1985) report to the Congress on the capital gains tax reductions of 1978, table 1.9, pp. 18–19.

Realizations also turned out to be negatively related to the level of nontraded wealth such as cash. If capital gains were often realized for consumption purposes, we would expect this result. When households have a great deal of cash and other liquid assets, they have less need to sell assets to finance consumption. The statistical results also suggest that a rise in the value of household wealth caused by rising asset prices induces more realizations, as expected.

These results were tested against a number of econometric specifications. The result was a range of estimates of the effect of tax rates from a 5.1% increase in realizations per point drop in tax rates to a 7.4% increase in realizations per point drop in tax rates. These results suggested a range of revenue maximizing capital gains tax rates of 13.5%–20%.

It is also likely that a good deal of any increased realization caused by a decrease in the tax rate is temporary. The data showed that the overall response of 6.2% more realizations per point of the tax rate was the combination of a first-year response of 8.4% per point and a long-run response of 5.4% per percentage point of the tax rate. This in turn implies that a long-run revenue-maximizing tax rate would be 18.5%.

The high responsiveness of capital gains realizations to tax rates is unlikely to be duplicated in other areas of the income tax. Taxed commodities such as labor supply will show comparatively little response to reductions in marginal tax rates because a relatively high proportion of the maximum possible level of supply is already in the market. By contrast, only a very small portion of existing capital gains are realized in a given year.

For example, total capital gains realized in 1982 amounted to a record $86.1 billion. But the revaluation in personally traded assets during that year alone was $306 billion, implying that realizations accounted for only 28.2% of that year's gains. In the high tax year of 1978, only $48.6 billion of gains were realized on total revaluations of $694 billion, or 7%. Clearly, the potential for increased realizations in 1978 was substantial. The large and growing stock of unrealized capital gains makes possible significant taxpayer responsiveness to the cost of realization. This in turn makes capital gains tax rates far more sensitive than other types of income.

Finally, it is important to stress that taxation of any commodity at its revenue-maximizing level is not optimal in any economic sense. The last dollars of revenue collected at the revenue-maximizing rate created enormous burdens on the economy relative to the extra dollars raised. The conclusions stated here can only be interpreted as implying that rates above the revenue-maximizing level are counterproductive.

References

Auten, G. 1979. *Empirical evidence on capital gains taxes and realizations.* Washington, D.C.: Office of Tax Analysis.

Auten, G., and C. Clotfelter. 1979. *Permanent vs. transitory effects and the realization of capital gains.* Washington, D.C.: Office of Tax Analysis.

Bailey, M. 1969. Capital gains and income taxation. In *The taxation of income from capital,* ed. A. C. Harberger and M. J. Bailey. Washington, D.C.: Brookings Institution.

Brame, B., and K. Gilmour. 1982. Sales of capital assets, 1973–1980. *Statistics of Income Bulletin* 2:28–39.

Brannon, G. 1974. The lock-in problem for capital gains: An analysis of the 1970–71 experience. In *The effect of tax deductibility on the level of charitable contributions and variations on the theme.* Washington, D.C.: Fund for Policy Research.

David, M. 1968. *Alternative approaches to capital gains taxation.* Washington, D.C.: Brookings Institution.

Feldstein, M., J. Slemrod, and S. Yitzhaki. 1980. The effects of taxation on the selling of corporate stock and the realization of capital gains. *Quarterly Journal of Economics* 94, no. 4 (June): 777–91.

———. 1984. The effects of taxation on the Selling of corporate stock and the realization of capital gains: Reply. *Quarterly Journal of Economics.*

Feldstein, M., and S. Yitzhaki. 1977. The effect of the capital gains tax on selling and switching of common stock. *Journal of Public Economics* (February).

Fredland, E., J. Gray, and E. Sunley. 1968. The six month holding period for capital gains: An empirical analysis of its effect on the timing of gains. *National Tax Journal* 21 (December): 467–78.

Kaplan, S. 1981. The holding period distinction of the capital gains tax. NBER Working Paper 762.

King, M., and D. Fullerton. 1984. *The taxation of income from capital.* Chicago: University of Chicago Press.

Lindsey, L. 1981. Is the maximum tax on earned income effective? *National Tax Journal* 34 (June): 249–56.

———. 1987. Capital gains: Rates, realizations, and Revenues. In *The effects of taxation on capital accumulation,* ed. Martin Feldstein. Chicago: University of Chicago Press.

Miller, M., and M. Scholes. 1978. Dividends and taxes. *Journal of Financial Economics* 6:333–64.

Minarik, J. 1981. Capital Gains. In *How taxes affect economic behavior,* ed. H. J. Aaron and J. A. Pechman. Washington, D.C.: Brookings Institution.

———. 1983. Professor Feldstein on capital gains—again. *Tax Notes* (May 9).

Poterba, J. 1985. How burdensome are capital gains taxes? MIT Working Paper 410. rev. ed., February 1986.

Stiglitz, J. 1969. The effects of income, wealth, and capital gains taxation on risk taking. *Quarterly Journal of Economics* 83:262–83.

U.S. Department of the Treasury. 1968–85. *Statistics of income 1965–82, individual income tax returns.* Washington, D.C.: Government Printing Office.

———. 1985. *Capital gains tax reductions of 1978.* Washington, D.C.: Office of Tax Analysis.

3 Corporate Capital Budgeting Practices and the Effects of Tax Policies on Investment

Lawrence H. Summers

The importance of depreciation and investment tax credit provisions in determining the level and composition of investment is widely recognized. Corporations carefully take account of depreciation tax benefits in their capital budgeting decisions. Therefore, economists analyze investment incentives by postulating that the present value of depreciation tax deductions along with the investment tax credit determines the effective purchase price of new capital goods, which in turn determines the cost of capital. Measures of the cost of capital are used widely in evaluating the likely effect of proposed tax reforms on the total level of investment and in assessing the distortions across capital goods caused by tax rules.

In both corporate investment decisions and economists' evaluations of tax policies, the present value of the depreciation deductions associated with specific investments plays a key role. Therefore, the choice of a discount rate to use in calculating this present value is fairly important. For example, the adverse effect of inflation in conjunction with historic cost depreciation on investment results from the increased discount rate that must be applied to future nominal depreciation allowances. At a zero discount rate, all depreciation schedules that permitted assets to be fully depreciated would be equal. It is only because

Lawrence H. Summers is a professor of economics at Harvard University and a research associate of the National Bureau of Economic Research.

This paper was prepared for the NBER Conference on Capital Taxation in Palm Beach, Florida, February 14–15, 1986. Deborah Mankiw helped in the design and dissemination of the survey reported in this paper and provided valuable comments. Andrei Shleifer and Jim Hines also provided helpful advice.

of discounting that depreciation schedules affect investment decisions, and their effects depend critically on the assumed discount rate.

Tax reform proposals often change the extent to which depreciation tax benefits are "backloaded." For example, Auerbach and Jorgenson's proposal (1981) would have given firms all of their depreciation benefits in the year that investments were made. On the other hand, the president's recent proposal (U.S. Treasury Department 1985) stretches out the tax benefits associated with investment outlays by indexing depreciation allowances and abolishing the investment tax credit. A comparison of either of these proposals with current law depends critically on the discount rate applied to future tax benefits in computing the cost of capital.

Despite its importance to both corporate decision making and economic analysis, the choice of an appropriate discount rate for depreciation allowances has received relatively little attention from tax analysts. This paper examines both theoretically and empirically the discounting of depreciation allowances and its implications for tax policy; I conclude that economic theory suggest that a very low and possibly negative real discount rate should be applied to future tax benefits. However, empirical evidence from a survey of 200 major corporations suggests that most companies use very high real discount rates for prospective depreciation allowances. This conflict makes alternative tax policies difficult to analyze. It surely suggests that there is little basis for confidence in tax policy assessments based on specific assumed discount rates that are constant across companies.

The paper is organized as follows. Section 3.1 argues that, given the risk characteristic of depreciation tax shields, a very low or negative real discount rate should be applied. Section 3.2 reports survey results on the actual capital budgeting practice of firms and discusses possible reasons for the apparent conflict between the recommendation of theory and firms' reported behavior. Section 3.3 concludes the paper by discussing the implications of the analysis for the assessment of alternative tax policies.

3.1   How Should Depreciation Allowances Be Discounted?

I begin by discussing the theory of capital budgeting and its application to the discounting of depreciation allowances. Economic theory provides clear guidelines as to how profit-maximizing corporations ought to treat future depreciation allowances. Because prospective depreciation allowances are very nearly riskless, they are more valuable than other prospective sources of cash flow. Safe cash flows, like the stream of future depreciation deductions, should be discounted at a lower rate than risky physical investments. The present value of depreciation deductions can then be used to assess potential investment projects. At current levels of inflation and interest rates, it appears that only a negligible real interest rate should be assumed in evaluating alternative tax policies.

In theory (and in practice, as demonstrated below), firms decide whether or not to undertake investments by computing the present value of the net cash flows they generate and using a discount rate corresponding to their cost of funds.[1] In a world of certainty, this process is completely straightforward. There is only one available rate of return, and firms invest to the point where the marginal project earns just this rate of return, that is, the net present value of the marginal project evaluated at the required rate of return is zero.

If a project is risky, the problem of capital budgeting becomes much more difficult. The normal procedure is to use a "risk-adjusted discount rate" appropriate to the project under consideration. In general, this rate will depend on the extent to which the project's returns move with aggregate returns in the economy. In the special case in which returns on a given project mirror the entire firm's returns, the appropriate discount rate may be inferred from the firm's stock market beta.

A fundamental principle in finance is that the valuation of a stream of cash flows is the same regardless of how it is divided into components. This insight shows how depreciation allowances should be treated, at least to a first approximation. Consider an arbitrary investment project. After an initial outlay, the project will generate a stream of uncertain future operating profits that then will be taxed. It will also generate a stream of future depreciation deductions that can be subtracted from the firm's income to reduce its tax liabilities. These two streams can be valued separately. It is difficult to value the profit stream without a satisfactory way to gauge its riskiness, but valuing future depreciation tax shields is much easier because they are close to riskless.[2] Therefore, they should be evaluated by using riskless discount rate. Since depreciation tax shields represent after-tax cash flows, they should be discounted at an after-tax rate of return. Then their present value can be added to the present value of the profit stream, evaluated at an appropriate risk-adjusted discount rate to calculate the total return on an asset.

The same conclusion follows from an arbitrage argument (as in Ruback 1987). Consider a set of prospective depreciation deductions that a firm may use. Imagine instead that the firm has a portfolio of Treasury bills designed so that the after-tax coupon payments in each period

---

1. For a general discussion of capital budgeting principles, see Brealey and Myers (1984).

2. The risk characteristics of depreciation tax shields are considered in a later section.

exactly equal the value of the tax deductions. It should be obvious that the firm has an equally valuable asset in either case. It follows that the appropriate discount rate for valuing depreciation deductions is the same as that for the Treasury bill portfolio: the after-tax nominal interest rate on safe assets. Note that the after-tax nominal interest rate is likely to be much lower than the appropriate discount rate for a project's operating cash flows.

Nominal interest rates on safe assets are currently less than 10%. With a corporate tax rate of 46%, corporations should discount future depreciation allowances at no more than a 5% nominal rate. This means a real rate very close to zero, at current levels of long-term expected inflation, rather than the 4% real rate assumed in many calculations of the effects of tax incentives.

So far, the assumption that prospective depreciation deductions represent a riskless asset has been maintained. In fact, though, future depreciation deductions are subject to some risks. Depreciation deductions will be useless for firms that have losses, become nontaxable, or are unable to use carryback and carryforward provisions. Auerbach and Poterba (1987) suggest that this is not an important factor for most large firms. There is also the possibility of changes in tax rules. Since depreciation deductions represent a hedge against changes in tax rates, this source of uncertainty may drive the appropriate discount rate down rather than up. Finally, there is the possibility that the depreciation rules will be changed with respect to assets already in place. This has never occurred in the United States. On balance, it seems fair to conclude that depreciation tax shields represent an essentially riskless asset.

The arguments made so far indicate that firms should discount expected operating profits and depreciation deductions separately at different rates. Firms might use a common discount rate for all the components of cash flow on a given project, reflecting their average degree of riskiness in some way, but this would not be correct: there is no way to know how much weight to give each component of cash flow until its value is determined, which in turn requires the choice of a discount rate. Even if an appropriate rate could be found, it would vary across projects depending on the value of prospective depreciation deductions. Moreover, a weighted average rate is unlikely to be varied when tax rules change and alter the share of a project's value represented by depreciation tax shields.

Before examining tax policies, I will report evidence on firms' actual capital budgeting practices. In general, they do not conform to those recommended in this section. The divergence between theory and corporate practice makes the analysis of tax policy difficult.

3.2   How Are Depreciation Deductions Discounted?

To learn how depreciation deductions are discounted by actual major corporations, a brief questionnaire was sent to the chief financial officers of the top 200 corporations in the Fortune 500. A copy of the questionnaire and cover letter are provided as an appendix to this paper. Usable replies were received from 95 corporations. No effort was made to raise the response rate by following up on the initial mailing, but there is little reason to suspect systematic differences in capital budgeting procedures between responding and nonresponding firms. The questionnaire was designed to find out whether capital budgeting procedures embodied the principles suggested in the preceding section and to find out what discount rates firms actually apply to depreciation deductions.

The survey results are reported in table 3.1. As the table indicates, the vast majority of corporate respondents stated that they had capital budgeting procedures and that these procedures were of "considerable" but not "overriding" importance in corporate investment decisions. Only 7% of the responding companies indicated that they discounted different components of cash flow on a given project at different rates, and even several of these companies did not distinguish operating profits and depreciation allowances. Many of the responding companies indicated that they dealt with risk issues by discounting projects emanating from different divisions or locations at different rates but that they discounted all the cash flows from a given project at the same rate. It is clear that the practice of separately discounting safe and unsafe components of a project's return, as suggested by theory, is a rarity in American industry.

Table 3.1   **Survey Results on the Discounting of Depreciation Allowances**

Capital budgeting procedure is of	
Overriding importance	6
Considerable importance	91
Little importance	3
Cash flow components discounted at different rates	6
Yes	94
No	
Discount rate applied to depreciation allowances	
< 12%	13
13%–15%	48
16%–18%	16
19%–21%	13
22% +	10

The lower part of the table indicates the distribution of the rates used by companies to discount depreciation allowances. In most cases, the figure refers to the common nominal discount rate applied to all cash flows. The reported discount rates for depreciation allowances were surprisingly high with a median of 15% and a mean of 17%, far in excess of the after-tax nominal interest rate. Given that depreciation tax shields have very similar risk characteristics across firms, it is also noteworthy that the rate at which they are discounted varies widely. The discount rates reported by firms varied 8%–30%. This variability is almost certainly the result of firms applying a common discount rate to all cash flows.

It is difficult to reconcile the level and variability of depreciation discount rates with the standard capital budgeting theory developed by financial economists and taught to practitioners. One explanation for the divergence between actual and recommended practice is that managers find the theory described earlier too complex to implement, given the benefits that can be expected. Another possibility is that managers fail to distinguish riskless and risky cash flows because shareholders do not make the distinction. In either event, analyzing tax policies using standard capital budgeting methods seems perilous. This issue is discussed in the next section.

3.3 Tax Policy Implications

This section treats two aspects of the relationship between tax policy and the discounting of depreciation allowances. First, I illustrate the sensitivity of judgments about the effects of alternative tax policies on incentives to the discount rate applied to future depreciation allowances. Second, I argue that the high and variable discount rates for depreciation used by firms may create important distortions themselves, which the tax structure may either mitigate or exacerbate.

Table 3.2 presents estimates of the sum of the present value of appreciation allowances and the deduction value of the investment tax credit under current tax law, the president's proposal of May 1985, and the House of Representatives' 1985 tax bill using alternative discount rates for depreciation.

Calculations indicate that the effects of alternative tax rules are quite sensitive to the assumed discount rate for depreciation allowances. At the theoretically appropriate zero real discount rate, only the House bill is less generous than a policy of immediate expensing of investment outlays. Current law provides a substantial subsidy to the purchase of new equipment because of the availability of the investment tax credit. On the other hand, with a 10% real discount rate applied to depreciation allowance, as suggested by the survey results, all three tax laws provide

Table 3.2   **Effects of Alternative Discount Rates on the Present Value of Depreciation Deductions under Alternative Proposals**

	ACRS Asset Class					
	I	II	III	IV	V	VI
$d = 0$						
Current law	1.06	1.08	1.08	1.08	.939	.736
President's proposal	1.00	1.00	1.00	1.00	1.00	1.00
House bill	.916	.890	.853	.807	.654	.624
$d = .1$						
Current law	.972	.938	.938	.938	.709	.487
President's proposal	.891	.862	.820	.759	.694	.351
House bill	.794	.741	.667	.583	.396	.366

Note: The present value of depreciation includes the value of the investment tax credit. A value of 1.0 corresponds to expensing. All calculations assume a 5% inflation rate. The discount rate is denoted by d.

benefits significantly less generous than expensing. Especially for long-lived equipment in asset class IV, both the Treasury bill and the House proposal would lead to a substantial increase in the effective purchase price.

The choice of a discount rate is especially important in evaluating the incentives provided for long-lived investments in structures. At a zero discount rate, the president's proposal provides far more incentives to structures investment than does current law. On the other hand, at a 10% rate, current law is more generous than the president's proposal.

The fact that firms use very high discount rates in evaluating projects suggests that the investment tax credit is likely to be a very potent tax incentive per dollar of government revenue forgone. The government should presumably trade off tax revenue at present and in the future using its borrowing rate. If firms discount future tax benefits at rates higher than the government borrowing rate, then tax incentives can be enhanced with no additional permanent cost to the government by restructuring tax incentives to move the benefits forward without changing the present value of the forgone revenue. The investment tax credit is frontloaded in this way. Still greater frontloading of tax incentives is possible through accelerating depreciation allowances, since this keeps the sum of the allowable deductions on an investment constant while increasing their present value. On the other hand, indexation of depreciation allowances tends to increase the duration of tax benefits.

The fact that firms use widely varying and inappropriate discount rates for depreciation allowances suggests that patterns of investment may be very substantially distorted in ways not considered in standard analyses of the effects of tax incentives. Certainly the returns demanded on marginal projects vary by much more across firms than do conventional measures of the cost of capital.

The reasons for these patterns are a potential subject for future research. One possible clue is that corporations and individuals seem to apply very different discount rates to depreciation allowances. The frequency with which individuals churn structures suggest that they apply a much lower (and more appropriate) discount rate than do corporations. This raises the possibility that agency issues may help to explain observed patterns of corporate capital budgeting. If so, then they may have an important bearing on the linkage between tax policies and investment decisions.

Appendix

Cover Letter

20 September 1985

Dear ———:

As part of its ongoing program of research on the economics of capital formation, the National Bureau of Economic Research is studying the effects of proposed reforms in the investment tax credit and tax depreciation schedules. The effects of alternative proposals depend critically on how taxes are factored into companies' capital budgeting procedures. I am therefore attempting to systematically gather information on major corporations' capital budgeting techniques.

I would be very grateful if you could fill in the enclosed questionnaire regarding your company's capital budgeting procedure, and return it in the enclosed envelope. Information identifying individual companies will not be presented in any of our research reports. I will of course furnish you with the results of the study when it is completed.

Thank you for your consideration.

Sincerely,

Lawrence H. Summers
Professor of Economics
Harvard University

LHS/mh
Enclosure

Questionnaire

1) Does your company use a capital budgeting procedure based on evaluations of the discounted cash flows from proposed projects? _____ yes _____ no

2) If yes, would you say that the present value of the cash flows from proposed projects is of _____ overriding importance
   _____ considerable importance
   _____ some consequence
   _____ little consequence
   in determining whether they are undertaken?

3) What is the hurdle rate of return you apply to new projects? Specifically in your capital budgeting procedure, what discount rate do you apply to the after tax nominal cash generated by the typical project? _____
   (Alternatively, please provide the real discount rate which you use and the expected inflation rate which enters your calculations.)

4) In evaluating projects some companies discount different components of cash flow at different rates because of their different risk characteristics. For example, some companies discount prospective depreciation tax shields at a low rate because there is not much uncertainty associated with them. Does your company treat different components of cash flow differently?
   _____ yes _____ no

5) If so, what discount rate do you apply to each of the following types of cash flow: _____ operating profits
   _____ scrap value
   _____ depreciation tax benefits
   _____ investment tax credits
   _____ rental income

Comments:

References

Auerbach, Alan, and Dale Jorgenson. 1980. Inflation-proof depreciation of assets. *Harvard Business Review* (September-October): 113–18.

Auerbach, Alan, and James Poterba. 1987. Tax loss carryforwards and corporate tax incentives. NBER Working Paper 1863. In *The effects of taxation on capital accumulation,* ed. Martin Feldstein. Chicago: University of Chicago Press.

Brealey, Richard, and Stewart Myers. 1984. *Principles of corporate finance.* New York: McGraw-Hill.

Jorgenson, Dale, and Robert Hall. 1967. Tax policy and investment behavior. *American Economic Review* 57 (June): 391–414.

Ruback, Richard S. 1987. Calculating the market value of riskless cash flows. *Journal of Financial Economics*. In press.

Summers, Lawrence H. 1987. Investment incentives and the discounting of depreciation allowances. In *The effects of taxation on capital accumulation*, ed. Martin Feldstein. Chicago: University of Chicago Press.

U.S. Department of the Treasury. 1985. *The president's tax proposals to the Congress for fairness, growth, and simplicity.*

4   The Tax Treatment of Structures

James R. Hines, Jr.

Structures constitute more than three-quarters of the U.S. tangible capital stock. Despite their relatively low rates of depreciation, structures account for more than half of all gross fixed investment in most years. Tax policies potentially have a major impact on both the level and composition of investment in structures. Two aspects of the taxation of structures—the relative burden placed on structures as opposed to equipment investment and the nontaxation of owner-occupied housing under the income tax—have attracted substantial attention in recent years. This paper explores these two aspects of the taxation of investments in structures.

The U.S. Department of the Treasury (1984), in its recent tax reform proposal, pointed to the extra tax burdens placed on structures relative to equipment as a major defect of the current Accelerated Cost Recovery System (ACRS). The 1985 Economic Report of the President echoes this sentiment, concluding, "The effective tax rate . . . is lower for equipment than for structures. Because different industries utilize different mixes of capital goods, differential taxation of assets results in differential taxation of capital income by industry. The average effective Federal corporate tax rate on fixed investment varies widely by industry." The decisions of the Congress in 1984 and 1985 to scale back the depreciation benefits to structures but not to equipment is perhaps surprising in the light of these conclusions.

The allegedly favorable treatment of owner-occupied housing has long been a target of academic critics of the tax system, although

James R. Hines, Jr. is an assistant professor of economics and public affairs at the Woodrow Wilson School, Princeton University and a faculty research fellow of the National Bureau of Economic Research.

suggestions for reform have generated little if any political support. The failure to include imputed rent is often treated as a tax subsidy. A large literature summarized in Rosen (1985) has estimated the welfare loss thought to come from tax-induced changes in tenure choice. And the corporate income tax is often opposed on the ground that it exacerbates the distortions caused by the nontaxation of owner-occupied housing.

While the tax system may well have a potent impact on the level and composition of the investment in structures, conventional analyses of this effect are very misleading. This paper reaches two main conclusions on the subject. First, under current tax law, certain types of investment in structures are very highly favored. Overall, it is unlikely that a significant bias toward equipment and against structures exists under current law. Second, the conventional view that the tax system is biased in favor of homeownership is wrong. Because of the possibility of "tax arbitrage" between high-bracket landlords and low-bracket tenants, the tax system has long favored rental over ownership for most households. The 1981 reforms, by reducing the top marginal tax rate, reduced this bias somewhat.

Many earlier analyses have reached different conclusions because of their failure to take account of several aspects of the behavior of real world investors who tend to reduce the effective tax burden on structures investment. First, structures may be depreciated more than once ("churned") for tax purposes. Particularly where devices can be found to reduce the effective rate of capital gains tax below the statutory rate, the effective purchase price of a structure may be substantially reduced by the knowledge that it can be depreciated several times. Second, some types of structures, particularly commercial buildings, are very easy to borrow against because they are quite liquid assets. To the extent that the tax system favors the use of debt finance they too will be favored. Third, certain types of investments, especially residential rental capital, facilitate tax arbitrage.

This paper is organized as follows. Section 4.1 reviews trends in structures investment over the past few years and highlights the dramatic increase in the rate of investment in commercial buildings that has occurred. Section 4.2 describes the tax rules on churning capital assets and considers under what circumstances churning will produce a tax advantage. Section 4.3 considers the role of leverage and raises the possibility that investments in structures are favored under current tax law because of their ability to carry debt. Section 4.4 examines the tax advantages to homeownership and shows that the tax law actually provides incentives for most households to rent their homes. Section 4.5 concludes by discussing the implications of these results for tax reform and for future research.

4.1 Patterns of Structures Ownership and Investment

A number of studies, notably Auerbach (1983) and Fullerton and Henderson (1984), have made rather elaborate calculations of the deadweight losses arising from the failure of the tax system to impose equal burdens on different types of corporate investment. In large part, the assumed differential taxation of equipment and structures drives the results of these studies. This differential taxation creates inefficiencies in production within industries and also favors some industries at the expense of others. Despite the results of many academic experts and of staff analyses suggesting that the then current law was heavily biased in favor of equipment, Congress in 1984 chose to scale back the depreciation benefits associated with investments in structures but not to alter the tax treatment of equipment investments. The 1984 action was taken at least in part because of a widespread perception that the 1981 acceleration of depreciation allowances had led to the rapid growth of tax shelters based on investments in structures.

How can one rationalize the perception that structures are a common tax shelter vehicle with calculations suggesting that they are among the most heavily taxed assets? Part of the answer may be found in the composition of the stock of structures in 1983, the most recent year for which data are available. Corporate structures represented less than a quarter of all structures in 1983 and less than half of all depreciable structures.

While detailed data are not available on the ownership of different types of structures, it is clear that the vast majority of residential capital is owner-occupied housing; the bulk of the remaining residential capital represents partnerships and proprietorships. Only a negligible fraction (2.5%) of residential capital is held in corporate form.

The ownership of nonresidential structures is more complex. It appears likely that most of the noncorporate structures are commercial buildings owned by partnerships or proprietors. The other main categories of nonresidential structures—industrial buildings, mines, and public utility structures—are probably largely owned by corporations.

4.1.1 Patterns of Structures Investment

Table 4.1 presents some information on the composition of structures investment in 1980 before the introduction of ACRS and in 1985. The table highlights some aspects of structures investment needed to assess neutrality arguments that suggest a tax bias against such investments. First, for a substantial share of structures investment, the effects of taxes cannot be analyzed sensibly in isolation. In 1985, for example, public utilities accounted for about 20% of all investment in structures. The profit rate of most public utilities is regulated; in many cases, the

Table 4.1   Structures Investment in 1980 and 1985 (Billions of Constant
                   1982 Dollars)

	1980	1985
Total Structures Investment	273.8	338.9
Nonresidential Structures	136.2	165.8
Industrial Buildings	16.0	14.2
Commercial Buildings	34.7	54.2
Office Buildings	15.3	28.3
Other	19.4	25.9
Education, Religious and Hospital	7.9	8.6
Mining and Petroleum	31.7	39.8
Public utilities	30.3	31.8
Farm structures	6.1	3.4
Other	9.5	13.8
Residential structures	137.6	173.1
Owner-occupied	60.7	95.3
Rental	76.9	77.8

Source: Unpublished data, Bureau of Economic Analysis, U.S. Department of Commerce.

benefits associated with tax incentives, especially the investment tax credit, are passed on to consumers.

About 40% of structures investment takes place in forms where other public microeconomic policies are involved in guiding the allocation of resources—educational and hospital buildings, mining and petroleum, and farming. Thus, as with the case of public utilities, examining the effects of tax benefits in isolation is likely to be very misleading.

For the remaining 40% of structures investment, in industrial and commercial buildings, tax considerations presumably are of primary importance. What is perhaps surprising, though, is that industrial buildings (plants) represent only about 10% of all nonresidential investments in structures. Commercial buildings account for the remaining 30% of nonresidential investment in structures.

Second, the table indicates that there has been a fairly dramatic shift in nonresidential investment in structures toward commercial buildings, and in particular office buildings, over the last five years. The dollar volume of investment in commercial buildings more than doubled between 1980 and 1985, compared with an increase of less than 50% in overall structures investment. The category of industrial buildings has been particularly weak over the same period, so investment in commercial buildings is now four times as great as investment in industrial buildings, compared with a ratio of two to one in 1980.

It is perhaps ironic that the 1981 tax cut, which had as a major objective spurring corporate investment, has been followed by a dramatic spurt in investment in commercial buildings, much of which is outside the corporate sector. Between 1980 and 1985, real investment in commercial structures increased by 56%; of that figure, office building investment rose 85%, while overall nonresidential construction increased only 22% and investment in equipment increased 26%. As discussed in detail later, the dramatic divergence between patterns of investment in commercial buildings and in other structures raises the suspicion that the tax system affects them very differently, despite their identical depreciation schedules.

Table 4.1 also indicates that residential investment has been surprisingly strong over the last five years: the dollar volume of residential investment has increased by more than 50%, and real investment in residential structures has increased by 26%, the same rate of growth as investment in equipment. Virtually all of the real growth in residential investment is attributable to owner-occupied housing, which has risen 57% despite the fact that it was the only type of structure to receive no new tax incentives in 1981.

4.2 Tax Churning of Nonresidential Real Property

As is now well understood, the present value of the depreciation allowance on a capital asset has an important impact on the incentive to invest in that asset. Indeed, differences in the treatment of depreciation among assets is often regarded as a major source of non-neutrality in the tax system. Unfortunately, calculation of the present value of the depreciation allowances on a given capital asset is not straightforward because the assets may be transferred and depreciated more than once for tax purposes. Particularly in an inflationary environment, there may be large advantages to turning assets over ("churning") to increase their depreciable basis. Even without inflation, asset sales raise the value of prospective depreciation allowances as long as those allowances are more accelerated than economic depreciation. However, the incentive to churn assets is mitigated by the capital gains taxes and "recapture" taxes that must be paid when depreciable assets are sold.

This section examines the effects on investment incentives of the possibility that assets can be depreciated more than once. After a review of the legal treatment of depreciation allowances and recapture, the section analyzes the desirability of churning different classes of assets. The results show the incentive to churn and the related incentive to invest to be rather sensitive to both tax rates and assumed discount rates.

4.2.1 Depreciation and Recapture Rules

The Economic Recovery Tax Act of 1981 established shorter and faster write-offs of capital costs for new investment in equipment and structures. The ACRS included a provision for depreciation of most classes of structures by a 175% declining balance method over fifteen years. The ACRS replaced the Asset Depreciation Range (ADR) system, which by comparison was far less generous in its treatment of capital depreciation allowances.

The 1981 tax law permits investors to choose from a variety of options for depreciating most classes of real property. Besides using 175% declining balance with switch-over to straight-line over an asset life of fifteen years, investors could select a straight-line depreciation method for an asset life of fifteen, thirty-five, or forty-five years as they chose. Under normal business circumstances, of course, an investor who planned never to sell his assets would always choose the shortest and most accelerated depreciation method. However, the recapture provisions of the law depend on the chosen method of asset depreciation.

For investors who choose straight-line depreciation and who sell their assets, the difference between the sales price and the tax basis is treated as a capital gain and is taxed at the capital gain rate. However, for investors in nonresidential structures who choose the 175% declining balance depreciation scheme and who sell their assets at a gain, the value of all depreciation allowances taken to date are recaptured as ordinary income (rather than as capital gains). This recapture of all past depreciation deductions normally is sufficiently costly that an investor would be better off using straight-line depreciation if he or she intended to sell the asset at any point.

Congress has modified the tax treatment of structures since passage of the 1981 act, although not substantially. The 1984 Deficit Reduction Act (DEFRA) lengthened the tax lives of most structures to eighteen years and slightly changed the tax treatment of installment sales. Tax lives of structures were further extended to nineteen years in 1985. Depreciation and recapture provisions were otherwise unaffected by these laws.

4.2.2 Evaluating the Incentive to Churn

The feasibility of churning an asset depends on its characteristics. A specialized industrial structure is likely to be difficult to sell because its functional specificity limits the range of potential buyers. It may also be difficult to sell and lease back because of the moral hazard and other problems associated with rental contracts. Most commercial real estate, on the other hand, is not highly specialized and is therefore easily leased. Indeed, Pan Am rents space in the Pan Am Building and Exxon rents its space in Rockefeller Center. A natural conjecture then is that, if the tax benefits to churning are substantial, a significant tax distortion may be created in favor of liquid assets. I explore this possibility by considering the magnitude of the tax incentive for the churning of commercial buildings.

Consider an investor, corporate or noncorporate, who invests in a commercial building in 1985, expecting that the tax law, inflation, and the interest rate will not change in the future. There are three possible depreciation strategies. First, the investor can use accelerated depreciation (with straight-line switch-over) and never churn the asset. Second, the investor can use accelerated depreciation and churn at the optimal point. Third, the firm can use straight-line depreciation and churn at the optimal point.

The potential tax benefits of churning are sensitive to the choice of capital gains tax rate. Previous calculations of the tax effects of asset sales have assumed that all capital gains are taxed upon realization at the statutory rate. Particularly for individuals, but to some extent for corporations as well, there are devices available that permit capital gains taxes to be avoided or deferred. This makes the churning of assets much more attractive. The features of the tax system that permit capital gains taxes to be avoided or reduced in present value include installment sales, variations in marginal tax rates, step-ups in basis, artificially generated losses, and outright cheating. Of these, the most important is probably the widespread use of installment sales, which delay and therefore reduce the real cost of capital gains taxes. These features are described in detail in Gordon, Hines, and Summers (1987).

The combination of these factors suggests that capital gains arising when structures investments are churned are effectively taxed at much less than the statutory rate. Therefore, the calculations also consider the incentives for churning that arise when individuals' capital gains are completely untaxed and when they are taxed at half the statutory rate, as well as corporations' incentives when their capital gains are taxed at half and three-quarters the statutory rate.

4.2.3   Results

Table 4.2 reports values of net before-tax corporate depreciation allowances and effective tax rates for representative parameter values, described in Gordon et al. (1987). The table presents results for investors with 2% required real rates of return. As Summers (1987) argues, if anything, this rate is higher than those suggested by theory but is rather lower than those actually used by corporations. This and other parameters used are standard in the literature on effective tax rates.

For the churning scenarios, it is assumed that the firm chooses the depreciation method and interval between asset sales so as to maximize profits. As this table makes clear, corporations will seldom want to churn structures for tax reasons under current law. This is hardly surprising, since the recapture provisions of the tax law were designed to prevent such transactions. If the marginal corporate investor faces less than the statutory capital gains rate, then it may become slightly preferrable to churn structures.

Table 4.2   Depreciation Benefits and Effective Tax Rates

| | Corporations: Depreciation Method | | | |
| | Accelerated Depreciation | Churning: Effective Capital Gains Rate | | |
Inflation Rate		0.14	0.21	0.28
3%	0.69	0.81	0.71	0.59
	(37%)	(26%)	(36%)	(44%)
6%	0.58	0.60	0.48	0.36
	(44%)	(43%)	(50%)	(55%)
10%	0.47	0.41	0.33	0.24
	(50%)	(53%)	(58%)	(59%)
	Individuals: Depreciation Method			
	Accelerated Depreciation	Churning: Effective Capital Gains Rate		
Inflation Rate		0.00	0.10	0.20
3%	0.69	1.06	0.90	0.75
	(41%)	(− 14%)	(18%)	(35%)
6%	0.58	0.85	0.68	0.53
	(48%)	(26%)	(42%)	(51%)
10%	0.47	0.69	0.48	0.36
	(54%)	(41%)	(54%)	(59%)

Note: Top entry is the present value of depreciation benefits; bottom entry in parentheses is the corresponding effective tax rate.

The bottom panel of table 4.2 presents similar calculations for top-bracket individuals who invest in structures through such devices as partnerships or proprietorships. As the table suggests, individuals have much stronger incentives to churn structures than corporations do. The top individual tax rate for ordinary income is 50%, and the top capital gains rate is 20%. Even ignoring the likely ability of individuals to avoid more of their capital gains liability than corporations, the 30% spread between the ordinary income and statutory capital gains rate is a much stronger incentive for churning than the 18% spread faced by corporations.

At a 3% rate of inflation, individuals always choose to churn their assets. If they can avoid capital gains taxes, they may face negative effective tax rates. Even at higher inflation rates, churning is a tax-preferred activity for individuals. Whether corporations or individuals face higher effective tax rates at a particular inflation rate may depend on their marginal capital gains rates. The source of funds matters as well, since the double taxation of corporate earnings may make the required corporate rate of return for new savings capital substantially

higher than the rate for, say, partnership investors. Section 4.3 treats
this issue in more depth, but it is sufficient at this point to note that
individuals may face strong incentives to invest in structures and sell
them later. In particular, these results suggest that the tax code favors
individual rather than corporate ownership of structures.

4.2.4 The Extent of Churning

The limited available empirical evidence suggests that churning is an
important part of the depreciation strategy for investors in structures.
Table 4.3 presents data on the depreciation methods chosen by corporations and partnerships for their structures investments in 1981 and
1982. Corporations used straight-line depreciation for 38% of the value
of their structures investments in 1981 and for 33% in 1982. Except in
very unusual circumstances, straight-line depreciation makes sense only
when firms plan to sell their assets at some date. In addition, under

Table 4.3   **Choice of Depreciation Method under ACRS (Millions of Current Dollars)**

	1981	1982
Corporations		
Total allocable fifteen-year real property other than low-income housing and public utility property	24,836	25,276
Accelerated depreciation	15,474	16,923
(%)	(62.3%)	(67.0%)
Straight-line	9,362	8,353
(%)	(37.7%)	(33.0%)
Unallocable property, foreign property, and tax-exempt organizations	6,171	5,294
Partnerships		
Total allocable fifteen-year real property other than low-income housing and public utility property	29,044	46,553
Accelerated depreciation	11,700	18,344
(%)	(40.3%)	(39.4%)
Straight-line	17,344	28,209
(%)	(59.7%)	(60.6%)
Unallocable property, foreign property, and tax-exempt organizations	1,879	1,492

Source: Unpublished preliminary data, Statistics of Income Division, Internal Revenue Service.

Note: Entries correspond to dollar values of fifteen-year real property (other than low-income housing and public utility structures) put in place and depreciated by the indicated method in these years. Unallocable property could not reliably be assigned to either the accelerated or straight-line depreciation category. These data exclude investments for which the IRS was unable to determine from the tax form which type of capital was being depreciated.

the generous pre-1984 recapture rules for installment sales, some firms may have used accelerated depreciation even if they wanted to churn their assets later. Through such extensive use of straight-line depreciation, the corporate sector gives up the substantial tax benefits of acceleration presumably in order to avoid costly recapture when the structures are sold later.

The bottom panel of table 4.3 presents far more striking information on partnerships. Fully 60% of the value of structures put in place by partnerships since the introduction of ACRS was depreciated straight-line. Of course, this is quite consistent with the finding that churning can be very attractive for individual investors and that individuals are more likely than corporations to take advantage of churning. The 60% figure in table 4.3 is likely to understate the extent of straight-line use for nonresidential investment, since the entry includes residential investment other than low-income housing. The absence of a special recapture penalty makes it very likely that partnerships use accelerated depreciation for their residential investments; the fraction of nonresidential structures depreciated straight-line is probably above 60%. The results in this section suggest that taking account of the attractiveness of tax churning may help to explain the recent boom in commercial building.

4.3   Corporate Financial Policy and the Effective Tax Rates on Structures Investment

So far, this analysis has considered features of the tax treatment of investments in structures that are common to individual investors, partnerships, and corporations. The current conventional wisdom that current tax law favors equipment over structures is derived from studies that have focused on corporate rather than overall investment. The calculations underlying these claims are almost always based on a variant of the formula for the user cost of capital derived by Hall and Jorgenson (1967). This formula, however, ignores a variety of factors, among them personal taxes and corporate financial policy. This section argues that, when the effects of personal taxes and corporate financial policy are taken into account, there is a much smaller difference between the calculated effective tax rates on structures and equipment and perhaps even a tax advantage to investments in structures.

The tax law seems to treat debt-financed investments favorably. Therefore, to the degree that a project can be financed with debt, it becomes more attractive. Investments in structures should be financed much more easily with debt than investments in equipment: structures are used as collateral for a loan easily, there is a dense secondary market for most types of buildings where a creditor can go if the collateral must be liquidated, and the market value of a building used as collateral is normally much more predictable than the values of many other assets. Therefore, a firm should be able to obtain a much larger loan on a building than on many other assets without imposing any effective default risk on the lender.

At the margin, corporations have a tax incentive toward debt finance. Corporate income is taxable both under the corporate tax and again, either as dividends or as capital gains, under the shareholders' personal income tax, while income accruing directly to shareholders is taxable only under the personal tax. For the same return, shareholders would thus prefer to loan money to the firm as debt rather than to purchase shares whose return is taxed twice. Corporate financing costs reflect this preference, so debt finance is less expensive.

In spite of this tax incentive to use debt finance, firms do not use debt exclusively because the possibility of bankruptcy leads to conflicts of interest between debt and equity holders, with associated real costs. There is every reason, however, to expect the optimal value of the debt-value ratio to vary by type of capital, for the reasons described above. It should also vary by industry, and observed debt-value ratios do. According to the figures reported in Fullerton and Gordon (1983) for a select group of industries in 1973, the observed debt-value ratios ranged from 0.08 in construction to 0.787 in real estate. The average in the economy was 0.399.

Given plausible parameter values and an assumed ability to finance new structures investments with 40% more debt than would be possible for equipment, the estimated effective tax rate on structures drops dramatically from 0.421 to 0.193. In contrast, the estimated effective tax rate on equipment reported by Auerbach (1983) for 1982 was 0.084. At least with these parameter values, the difference becomes minor. These results are sensitive to the choice of interest rate, debt-value ratio, and tax rates for marginal investors. Gordon et al. (1987) describe the calculations, which show effective tax rates to be as low as 7% in other realistic scenarios.

4.4 Taxation and Tenure Choice

It is widely believed that the tax system favors owner-occupied housing. This conclusion is repeated in many textbooks and forms the basis for much research on the effects of taxation on tenure choice. The standard argument is straightforward. The services of owner-occupied housing are untaxed while rental payments are treated as taxable income. While landlords are permitted tax deductions that are not permitted to homeowners, as long as there is some positive effective tax rate on rental income, home ownership is nonetheless thought to be tax favored. As a number of authors, including Litzenberger and Sosin (1977), Titman (1982), and Hendershott (1987), have recognized, there is an important defect in this argument. It ignores the possibility of tax arbitrage between high-bracket landlords and low-bracket tenants. High-bracket taxpayers have a comparative advantage over low-bracket taxpayers in making use of interest deductions that they can exploit by borrowing in order to buy real estate that they then rent to low-bracket taxpayers.

When this effect is recognized, it turns out that homeownership is tax favored for only a small number of taxpayers. This section demonstrates that conclusion by considering the effects of homeownership in a setting where people would be indifferent between owning and renting their homes except for tax incentives. In reality, of course, other considerations such as transaction costs, desire to own one's own place of residence, and the differing incentive effects of rental and ownership contracts influence tenure choice. But in order to study the incentives provided by the tax system, the calculations abstract from these effects.

It is straightforward to calculate the costs of owner-occupied and rental housing. I assume that competition forces rents down to the point where landlords earn the same risk-adjusted return on rental property as they could on bonds. This assumption is warranted as long as landlords can borrow or lend at the margin. It will become apparent that top-bracket landlords will be able to charge the lowest rents and so represent the marginal supplier of rental housing.

Under ACRS, residential property was permitted 175% declining balance depreciation over a useful life of fifteen years (now nineteen years). In addition, residential property has the desirable feature that accelerated depreciation is recaptured upon sale at ordinary income rates only to the extent that it has exceeded straight-line depreciation. The 1981 act also permits purchasers of used assets to use the 175% declining balance depreciation method. Prior to 1981, asset lives were substantially longer, but investors in new residential structures were allowed 200% declining balance (or sum-of-the-years-digits) depreciation. Purchasers of used assets were required to use 125% declining balance depreciation, thereby lowering the prices of used structures relative to new structures, and reducing the value of tax churning. High marginal tax rates on individuals provided ample incentive for investment in rental housing, however.

Table 4.4 presents values of marginal tax rates for individuals who were indifferent between homeownership and renting for the years 1965–85. The results in table 4.4 describe four scenarios. I examine cases in which individuals who own rental housing avoid half their capital gains liability at the margin and cases in which they pay the full

Table 4.4   **Tenure Choice and Tax Status, 1965–85 (%)**

| | | Minimum Tax Bracket for Owner-Occupiers | | | |
| | | Full Capital Gains Liability | | One-Half Capital Gains Liability | |
Year	Maximum Personal Tax Bracket	Risky Returns	Riskless Returns	Risky Returns	Riskless Returns
1965	70	0	64	0	70 +
1970	73	24	62	27	69
1975	70	59	59	59	59
1980	70	55	63	56	64
1981	69	53	56	53	56
1982	50	32	50 +	41	50 +
1983	50	28	50	38	50 +
1984	50	19	34	37	44
1985	50	11	23	13	29

Note: Entries correspond to break-even tax rates for tenure choice. Taxpayers with lower marginal tax rates will be renters, and those with higher marginal rates will be owner-occupiers.

statutory rate on capital gains. In addition, I separately report specifications in which investors treat depreciation allowances as risky and in which they are viewed as riskless.

The striking implication of the findings reported in table 4.4 is that home ownership has not been favored by the tax code until recently. High individual tax rates before 1982 encouraged most taxpayers to rent their dwellings from top-rate individuals. While the results in table 4.4 reflect changing inflation and interest rates as well as statutory tax changes. The conclusion that falling personal taxes have undone changes in the depreciation provisions to make homeownership much more attractive in recent years is inescapable. From this perspective, it is perhaps not surprising that home ownership and residential investment have been strong in recent years.

4.5 Conclusions

This paper highlights the difficulty of predicting the effects of tax rules on the level and composition of investment. The incentives for investment in the tax law turn out to depend on a number of quite specific features of the law, rather than just on tax rates and depreciation schedules. They also depend on how the tax law interacts with the liquidity characteristics of different types of assets. Analyses that omit these factors are likely to have little predictive power for the effects of tax changes on the composition of investment. Moreover, normative conclusions based on models that omit these factors are likely to be very misleading.

This paper implies that there are at most minimal allocative losses resulting from the differential treatment of equipment and structures under current depreciation schedules. There are substantial reasons to believe that residential and nonresidential real estate investments made by partnerships are substantially favored under current law, because of the tax advantages associated with churning assets, leverage, and arbitrage between taxpayers in different brackets.

References

Auerbach, Alan J. 1983. Corporate taxation in the United States. *Brookings Papers on Economic Activity,* no. 2, pp. 451–506.

Fullerton, Don, and Roger H. Gordon. 1983. A reexamination of tax distortions in general equilibrium models. In *Behavioral simulation methods in tax policy analysis,* ed. Martin Feldstein. Chicago: University of Chicago Press.

Fullerton, Don, and Yolanda Henderson. 1984. Incentive effects of taxes on income from capital: Alternative policies in the 1980s. In *The legacy of Reaganomics: Prospects for long term growth,* ed. Charles R. Hulton and Isabel V. Sawhill. Washington, D.C.: Urban Institute Press.

Gordon, Roger H., James R. Hines, Jr., and Lawrence H. Summers. 1987. Notes on the tax treatment of structures. NBER Working Paper 1896. In *The effects of taxation on capital accumulation,* ed. Martin Feldstein. Chicago: University of Chicago Press.

Hall, Robert E., and Dale W. Jorgenson. 1967. Tax policy and investment behavior. *American Economic Review* 57:391–414.

Hendershott, Patric H. 1987. Tax changes and capital allocation in the 1980s. In *The effects of taxation on capital accumulation,* ed. Martin Feldstein. Chicago: University of Chicago Press.

Litzenberger, Robert, and Howard Sosin. 1977. Taxation and the incidence of home ownership across income groups. *Journal of Finance* 32:261–75.

Rosen, Harvey. 1985. Housing subsidies: Effects on housing decisions, efficiency, and equity. In *Handbook of public economics,* ed. A. Auerbach and M. Feldstein, vol. 1. Amsterdam: North-Holland.

Summers, Lawrence H. 1987. Investment incentives and the discounting of depreciation allowances. In *The effects of taxation on capital accumulation,* ed. Martin Feldstein. Chicago: University of Chicago Press.

Titman, Sheridan D. 1982. The effect of anticipated inflation on housing market equilibrium. *Journal of the American Real Estate and Urban Economics Association* 37:827–42.

U.S. Department of the Treasury. 1984. *Tax reform for fairness, simplicity, and economic growth: The Treasury Department report to the president* (November). Washington, D.C.: U.S. Department of the Treasury.

5 Tax Reform and the Slope of the Playing Field

Patric H. Hendershott

One goal of tax policy is the efficient allocation of resources. From the perspective of real capital, efficiency translates into the familiar "level playing field" on which different forms of capital investment would compete on equal terms. A relevant question then is, would the changes in tax rates and tax incentives embodied in the Treasury, administration, and House (HR 3838) reform plans and, most importantly, the Tax Reform Act of 1986 render the field more level? Because the slope of the playing field under pre-1986 law also depends on the level of inflation, a related question is, would this slope's sensitivity to inflation be dampened or exaggerated by the reforms? Providing answers to these questions is the purpose of this paper. Along the way, I also take a brief look backward at the impact of early 1980 tax changes.

Only the administration plan would create a more level playing field (a full version of this analysis is contained in Hendershott 1987). The Treasury plan, the House bill, and the 1986 Act all would tilt the existing field toward owner-occupied housing, the investment that is already most tax favored. In effect, we would return to the pre-1981 world. The administration plan and 1986 Act, and the House bill to a lesser extent, would also significantly reduce the sensitivity of the playing field to inflation. The Treasury plan, in contrast, would increase this sensitivity, in spite of its professed intent to do otherwise.

5.1 The Annual Rental Cost and the Efficient Allocation of Capital

A key determinant of investment in any type of capital good is its annual rental cost. If the gross return from investment promises to

Patric H. Hendershott is a professor of finance at Ohio State University and a research associate of the National Bureau of Economic Research.

exceed this cost, then investment will occur. Because additional investment drives down the gross return, an equilibrium eventually will be reached where the gross return from new investment equals the rental cost. Moreover, the higher the rental cost for any capital good, the higher the required gross return will be and thus the less investment there will be in the good in equilibrium.

In a world devoid of taxes and tax incentives, the annual rental cost or investment hurdle rate is simply the real interest rate, including the risk premium relevant to the asset, plus economic depreciation. The higher the risk premium an asset must promise and the greater its anticipated rate of depreciation, the higher the hurdle rate and thus the required gross return. But this is only appropriate: assets that are riskier and wear out faster should promise greater returns to compensate for their greater risk and more rapid deterioration. The zero-tax and no-tax-incentive world would yield a level playing field, that is, one in which the risk-adjusted net (of depreciation) rental costs for all investments are equal.

But our world has numerous taxes and tax incentives. The "effective tax rates" for alternative investments, plus differences in the financing and riskiness of the investments, tilt the playing field in various directions. The tilts, in turn, cause overinvestment in some capital goods and underinvestment in others. The result is a lower average return on capital than would exist with the optimal allocation of capital and a reduction in the national standard of living. This reduction is labeled an efficiency loss.

5.2 The Playing Field under Pre-1986 Law

Table 5.1 lists the risk-adjusted net rental costs for seven capital classes and five tax regimes: pre-1986 law; the November 1984 Treasury plan; the May 1985 administration plan; HR 3838, passed in December 1985; and the Tax Reform Act of 1986, enacted in the fall of 1986. There are four corporate asset classes (inventories, equipment, public utility structures, and industrial structures) and three noncorporate real estate assets (depreciable rental and commercial structures, owner-occupied housing of households with adjusted gross incomes under $50,000 in 1985 dollars, and owner-occupied housing of households with incomes over $50,000). The calculations for pre-1986 law assume a 5% inflation rate and a 10% debt rate and have been adjusted to the presumed risk of owner-occupied housing. Other important assumptions will be noted.

As is shown, the adjusted net rental costs, or investment hurdle rates, vary widely across corporate assets under pre-1986 law. Inventories have the highest costs; utilities and, especially, equipment have the lowest. The differences are explained easily. Inventories are subject to

Table 5.1   Risk-adjusted Net Rental Costs: 5% Inflation

	Pre-1986 Law	Treasury Plan	Administration Plan	House Bill	Tax Reform Act of 1986
Corporate investments					
Inventories	.109	.074	.086	.083	.085
Equipment	.036	.068	.051	.063	.061
Public utilities	.060	.072	.048	.072	.070
Structures	.075	.073	.064	.070	.073
Depreciable real estate	.041	.041	.036	.040	.039
Owner-occupied housing					
Under $50,000 AGI	.035	.020	.035	.026	.025
Over $50,000 AGI	.016	.012	.023	.010	.014
Level of interest rates	.100	.074	.094	.087	.086

Source: Except for the calculations for the Tax Reform Act of 1986, these numbers are based on Hendershott (1987).

a special inflation tax because of FIFO (first-in, first-out) accounting; utilities and equipment benefit from a special tax break, the investment tax credit. Because a given percentage credit is more beneficial as the life of the asset is shorter, the credit lowers the cost for equipment more than the cost for utilities.

The hurdle rate for depreciable real estate structures is far less than that for corporate industrial structures. In addition to the double taxation of corporate income, discrimination in the current system against riskier, more equity-financed investments and the lower risk and greater debt associated with real estate investments cause this difference.[1] More specifically, the calculations are based on a one-third debt-to-value ratio and a 5% risk premium for corporate investments, versus a two-thirds debt-to-value ratio and 2.5% risk premium for depreciable real estate.

The hurdle rates for owner-occupied housing are the lowest, reflecting the absence of taxation on the returns from this asset. (These calculations are independent of the assumed risk premium and, under

1. These calculations are somewhat controversial because the impacts of double taxation and the riskiness of investments on relative hurdle rates are uncertain. If the personal tax rate on share returns is taken to be a 40/60 weighted average of the tax rates on dividends and capital gains, the 40 reflecting the percentage of real corporate earnings that historically have been paid out, then double taxation causes a large wedge in hurdle rates. In contrast, if a 10/90 weighted average is employed, reflecting the proportion of equity capital raised by new share issues rather than from retained earnings, the wedge is much smaller (Auerbach 1983, 918–26). Similarly, if one accepts the analysis of Bulow and Summers (1984), risk creates a large wedge, but this is not true under the framework of Gordon and Wilson (1986). An intermediate wedge, based upon a 10/90 dividend/capital gains tax assumption and the Bulow-Summers analysis, is built into the estimates in table 5.1.

pre-1986 law, are largely independent of the assumed loan-to-value ratio.) The advantage of nontaxation is, of course, greater as the tax bracket of the homeowner rises. For simplicity, owners have been divided into only two classes, those with incomes above $50,000 and those below $50,000. The hurdle rates for these classes are rough weighted averages of owners within each of these classes; the weights depend on the relative quantities of housing that the owners demand.

A comparison of the risk-adjusted net costs under pre-1986 law suggests two ways to produce a more level playing field. First, the general advantage of real estate, especially owner-occupied housing of higher-income households, can be lessened. (While a plausible case can be made for tax incentives to encourage homeownership, a persuasive case for subsidizing owners to occupy larger houses has not been made.) Second, the disparity of costs across corporate assets can be reduced. The latter suggestion mostly requires lowering the costs of other corporate assets to that of equipment; the often-noted bias in favor of equipment under pre-1986 law, while large relative to other corporate investments, is small relative to capital investments in general.

5.3 The Treasury, Administration, and House Tax Reforms

Proposed tax reforms generally treat capital income less favorably than did pre-1986 law: the investment tax credit is dropped in all proposals, depreciation allowances are less generous in most cases, and the tax rate at which real estate expenses are deductible would decline under every reform. As a result, aggregate investment demand would fall if the existing level of interest rates continued. I have constructed a model in which the interest rate declines just enough to maintain the demand for aggregate investment. This interest rate level is shown at the bottom of table 5.1, and the adjusted net rental costs listed in the table for the various reforms are based on the new lower level. This procedure makes the general level of adjusted net costs in any column comparable to that in any other column. If the costs were computed with the initial 10% level of interest rates, then all the numbers in each column would be increased. The further 10% is above the interest rate in the bottom row, the larger would be the increase. However, the relationship among the numbers in any column—the slope of the playing field—would change little for the administration and House reforms, and the differences across the numbers for the Treasury plan would be even greater.

The Treasury plan attempts to neutralize the tax system for inflation by indexing everything. Only real capital gains, including those on inventories, would be taxed; depreciation would be on a replacement, rather than historic, cost basis; and only the "real" part of interest expense would be taxed and could be deducted (except all mortgage interest on one's principal residence would remain deductible). The Treasury plan also attempts to tax all assets and business forms (except owner-occupied housing) equally. To this end, tax depreciation for each depreciable asset would equal the Treasury's best estimate of true economic depreciation. The investment tax credit would be dropped. Real capital gains would be taxed at the regular income tax rate, and half of corporate dividends would be deductible at the corporate level. As the data in table 5.1 show, the indexation of inventory gains, the removal of the tax credit, and the proposed treatment of tax depreciation would vastly narrow the risk-adjusted net costs across corporate assets. Also, the partial dividend exclusion would reduce the double taxation of corporate investments.

While the Treasury plan scores high in reducing the disparities across corporate investments—and in reducing the disparities across industries within the corporate sector, although that point is not illustrated here—the plan fails to reduce the advantages of real estate. In fact, the relative advantage of owner-occupied housing rises by nearly 25%. Under pre-1986 law, the difference between the average net costs for corporate and owner-housing capital is about four percentage points (0.067–0.026); with the Treasury plan, the difference rises to 5.25 percentage points (0.069–0.016). Because owner-occupied housing is currently the most tax-favored asset, the added efficiency loss from enlarging this bias swamps the efficiency gain from better allocation across corporate assets.[2]

The administration plan retreats from the general principles of the Treasury plan in significant respects: all interest would continue to be deductible; investors in nondepreciable assets would have the option of paying taxes on nominal capital gains at half of the regular income tax rate; tax depreciation would exceed economic depreciation; only one-tenth of dividends would be deductible; and, in order to make the plan revenue neutral, inventory gains would continue to be nonindexed. Tax depreciation would be especially generous for equipment that continues to be classified as three or five years and for public utility struc-

2. These conclusions regarding the Treasury plan differ from those of Fullerton and Henderson (1987), who find that the relative advantage to owner-occupied housing would rise only half as much. The differences in the two studies are largely attributable to different assumptions about home mortgage financing. Because mortgage interest expense would be fully deductible but mortgage (bond) interest income would be only partially taxed, I have assumed that households would raise their loan-to-value ratios from 67% to 85%. The gain from this pure tax arbitrage—issuing mortgage debt and investing in GNMA securities—is an effective reduction in the rental cost of owner housing, whose collateral is needed for the arbitrage. Fullerton and Henderson assume a base case loan-to-value ratio of only 33% and no increase in response to the Treasury plan. (When I analyze the Treasury plan with full interest indexation—home mortgage interest, too, is only partially deductible—the relative advantage to owner-occupied housing increases by only one-third percentage point.)

tures; allowable depreciation would exceed that under pre-1986 law even at zero inflation. However, most five-year equipment would be reclassified as six-, seven-, and even ten-year equipment. As a result, biases against inventories and in favor of equipment would remain, although at much reduced levels. Moreover, the administration plan would reduce the general bias against corporate investments and in favor of owner-occupied housing, especially of higher-income households. Overall, the result would be a more level playing field and more efficient allocation of capital.

The House bill removes the investment tax credit and substantially lengthens depreciation schedules for structures. The resulting impact on adjusted net rental costs would be remarkably similar to that of the Treasury plan. Moreover, because far less base broadening would occur than under the Treasury and administration plans (most important, state and local taxes would continue to be fully deductible), marginal tax rates for most homeowners with incomes between $40,000 and $90,000 would not decline relative to current law (Hendershott and Ling 1986); thus, neither would the absolute advantage of owner-occupied housing. The disparity among corporate net rental costs would narrow sharply, but these costs would be at a high level, while costs for owner-occupied housing would decline from their already low levels. Again, a generally less level field and less efficient allocation of capital would result.

5.4 The Tax Reform Act of 1986

The capital provisions of the enacted legislation are quite similar to those of the House bill: the investment tax credit is removed and the tax depreciation schedules for structures are substantially lengthened. The main differences between the House bill and the 1986 Tax Act are base broadening on the personal side (lost sales tax and consumer interest deductions, lost capital gains exclusion, limited exclusions for IRA and SRA (401k) contributions, etc.) and lower marginal tax rates, especially for high income households.

Given the basic similarities between the House and the enacted bills, the adjusted net rental costs are quite comparable. The only noteworthy difference is a nearly half percentage point higher rental cost for owner-occupied housing of high income households under the Tax Reform Act of 1986. Their higher cost stems from their lower marginal tax. Because this capital category is the most tax-favored, a higher cost leads to a more efficient allocation of capital. Still, the playing field will be less level than under pre-1986 law and thus capital allocation will be less efficient.

5.5   What ERTA/TEFRA Wrought

The Economic Recovery Tax Act of 1981 (ERTA) roughly halved depreciation tax lives. Together with the existing investment tax credit, this created negative effective tax rates on equipment. However, the Tax Equity and Fiscal Responsibility Act of 1982 (TEFRA), which reduced the depreciable base for equipment by one-half the investment tax credit (and reneged on the more accelerated depreciation methods promised in 1985), got the tax rates back into the positive zone. Because ERTA/TEFRA were so maligned for the biased (toward equipment) playing field they created (see, e.g., Gravelle 1982), it is perhaps useful to revisit the impact of the early 1980 tax changes.

Table 5.2 shows risk-adjusted net rental costs both before and after ERTA/TEFRA. The expected long-run inflation rate at the time of enactment is presumed to have been 8%, and the level of interest rates associated with that is taken to be 13%. Comparing the pre- and post-ERTA/TEFRA numbers, we do see a marked reduction in the hurdle rate for equipment relative to other corporate investments: 3.5 percentage points vis-à-vis inventories, two percentage points relative to public utilities, and one percentage point more than structures. On the other hand, what had been a large bias in favor of owner-occupied housing was sharply reduced. The "average" gap between hurdle rates on corporate capital and owner-occupied housing was lowered from roughly six percentage points (0.07 less 0.01) to about 3.5 percentage points (0.06 less 0.025).

Therefore, ERTA/TEFRA reduced the efficiency of the allocation within the corporate sector but increased the efficiency of allocation between owner-occupied housing and the corporate sector. Given the large bias toward owner-occupied housing prior to ERTA/TEFRA, overall capital would likely be allocated more efficiently post- than pre-

Table 5.2   **Risk-adjusted Net Rental Costs: 5% Inflation Rate**

	Pre-ERTA	Post-ERTA/TEFRA
Corporate investments		
Inventories	.100	.110
Equipment	.054	.030
Public utilities	.063	.057
Structures	.079	.066
Depreciable real estate	.039	.039
Owner-occupied housing		
Under $50,000 AGI	.025	.036
Over $50,000 AGI	.001	.013
Level of Interest Rates	.130	.141

ERTA/TEFRA. The principal deficiency of the Treasury plan, the House bill, and the enacted legislation, from the capital efficiency perspective, is their tendency to reestablish the large bias in favor of owner-occupied housing (compare the net adjusted hurdle rate for owner-occupied housing in tables 5.1 and 5.2).

5.6 Inflation Neutrality

The inflation neutrality of the various tax regimes is calculated by computing the changes in the adjusted net rental costs that would occur as inflation rises from zero to 10%. The change in the level of interest rates accompanying the 0.10 rise in inflation is listed in the last row of table 5.3. Under pre-1986 law (and the administration and House reforms), interest rates rise by about 1.4 times the increase in inflation because nominal, rather than real, interest is taxed and deducted. With the 1.4 increase, the general level of rental costs that evolves maintains aggregate investment. With perfect interest indexation (the taxation and deduction of real interest only), interest rates would rise one-for-one with the increase in inflation. The rate increase is 1.15-for-one under the Treasury plan because two flaws in its indexation feature would continue to allow deduction of part of the inflation premium in interest rates. First, the indexation presumes a 6% real interest rate, a level that is probably too high even under pre-1986 tax law and would certainly be far too high after interest rates declined in response to the adoption of indexation. Second, mortgage interest expense on one's principal residence would continue to be fully deductible under the Treasury plan.

Table 5.3   **Change in Risk-adjusted Net Rental Costs as Inflation Rises from 0% to 10%**

	Pre-1986 Law	Treasury Plan	Administration Plan	House Bill
Corporate investments				
Inventories	.017	.018	.030	.023
Equipment	.016	.017	.003	.014
Public utilities	.011	.018	.003	.009
Structures	.005	.018	.003	.007
Depreciable real estate	− .015	.004	− .011	− .007
Owner-occupied housing				
Under $50,000 AGI	.012	− .005	.013	.008
Over $50,000 AGI	− .015	− .021	− .005	− .013
Change in level of interest rates	.146	.115	.145	.139

Two sources of bias in pre-1986 tax law, the advantage of debt and the double-taxation disadvantage of corporate ownership, are aggravated by inflation. Thus, inflation favors depreciable real estate and high-income owner-occupied housing, both of which are heavily debt financed and not corporate owned, and disfavors corporate investments that are heavily equity financed. Lower-income owner housing is also disfavored because the owners deduct interest at a low tax rate and do not have an advantage from debt financing. With a marginal tax rate of 0.2, the real after-tax rate rises from 2.5% at a zero inflation rate to 4% at a 10% rate. In contrast, with a 0.4 tax rate, the real after-tax rate would decline from 1.75% to 0.5%.

Full interest indexation and integration of corporate and personal taxes would eliminate the disadvantages to both equity finance and corporate ownership. Because exaggeration of these biases is the source of inflation non-neutrality under pre-1986 law, one would expect the Treasury plan to be more inflation neutral than pre-1986 law. Unfortunately, imperfections in the Treasury plan, particularly the exclusion of home mortgage interest expense from the indexation provision, render the plan more sensitive to inflation. While the large advantage to depreciable real estate is removed, the advantage to owner-occupied housing is increased. With the much smaller increase in nominal interest rates and the continued full deductibility of interest payments, the real after-tax mortgage rate declines as inflation accelerates, even for owners in the 0.2 tax bracket. The other side of the coin is higher costs for corporate investments. However, the different types of corporate investment are affected equally (badly) by inflation.

The administration plan, in contrast, would be more inflation neutral than pre-1986 law. The two inflation-favored investments under pre-1986 law, depreciable real estate and owner-occupied housing of high-income households, would be less favored. This follows from the reduction in tax rates that lowers the advantage of debt. With the exception of inventories, which would still be subject to the inflation tax, corporate costs would be insensitive to inflation. (This would also be true of inventory costs if revenue neutrality had not caused the inflation tax to be maintained.)

The House bill, too, would reduce the inflation biases existing in pre-1986 law, although by less than the administration plan. Again, the two most inflation favored investments under pre-1986 law would be less favored, but the increase in the cost for high-income owner-occupied housing is limited. The small increase relative to the administration plan follows from differences in the marginal tax rate at which owners in the $50,000–$100,000 income range would deduct mortgage interest. Under the House bill, this tax rate would rise by two percentage points, tending to lower the after-tax mortgage rate; in contrast, this tax rate would decline by 6.5 percentage points under the administration plan.

The 1986 Tax Act, which has not been formally analyzed, would be slightly less neutral than the administration plan but more neutral than the House bill and pre-1986 law.

5.7 Conclusion

Possible benefits of tax reform include faster economic growth and greater equity. A part of economic growth is the channeling of saving into the most productive real investments. The ability of various tax regimes to channel saving efficiently and independently of the inflation rate has been the focus of this paper.

On the basis of this single criterion, the May 1985 administration proposal is superior to pre-1986 law, the Treasury proposal of November 1984, HR 3838 passed by the U.S. House of Representatives in December 1985, and the Tax Reform Act of 1986. Efficient capital investment requires that the risk-adjusted net (of depreciation) rental costs of all capital goods be equal. The administration plan would reduce both the disparity of these costs across corporate investments and the gap between the average costs for corporate investments and owner-occupied housing. While the Treasury plan, the House bill, and the enacted 1986 law would all narrow the differences in rental costs across corporate assets even more than the administration plan would, these reforms would greatly increase the bias in favor of owner-occupied housing. In fact, this bias is likely to be as great as it was prior to ERTA. As a result, saving would be allocated even less efficiently under these plans than under pre-1986 law.

References

Auerbach, Alan J. 1983. Taxation, corporate financial policy and the cost of capital. *Journal of Economic Literature* 21 (September): 905–40.

Bulow, Jeremy I., and Lawrence H. Summers. 1984. The taxation of risky assets. *Journal of Political Economy* 92: 20–39.

Fullerton, Don, and Yolanda Henderson. 1987. The impact of fundamental tax reform on the allocation of resources. In *The effects of taxation on capital formation,* ed. Martin Feldstein. Chicago: University of Chicago Press.

Gordon, Roger H., and J. D. Wilson. 1986. Measuring the efficiency cost of taxing risky capital income. NBER Working Paper 1992.

Gravelle, Jane. 1982. Effects of the 1981 depreciation revisions on the taxation of income from business capital. *National Tax Journal* 35 (March): 1–20.

Hendershott, Patric H. 1987. Tax changes and capital allocation in the 1980s. NBER Working Paper 1911. In *The effects of taxation on capital accumulation,* ed. Martin Feldstein. Chicago: University of Chicago Press.

Hendershott, Patric H., and D. C. Ling. 1986. Likely impacts of the administration proposal and the House bill. In *Tax reform and real estate.* ed. James Follain. Washington, D.C.: Urban Institute Press.

6   Tax Rules and Business Investment

Martin Feldstein

The current proposals to eliminate the investment tax credit and to modify other aspects of business taxation have brought renewed attention to the question of how sensitive business investment is to changes in tax rules. Critics of the tax changes proposed by the administration and of those enacted by the House of Representatives charge that they would significantly depress productive investment in business plant and equipment. The defenders of these proposals argue in reply that investment is relatively insensitive to tax rules, depending instead on capacity utilization and business confidence.

This paper reviews new statistical evidence that the share of gross national product (GNP) devoted to net investment in plant and equipment is quite sensitive to tax-induced changes in the profitability of such investment.[1] The specific quantitative analysis implies, for example, that the tax bill passed by the House of Representatives in December 1985 would reduce overall net investment in plant and equipment by approximately 10%, with larger reductions in equipment and smaller reductions in investment in structures. Over time, this reduction in net investment would reduce the capital stock and gross investment by even larger percentages. As a result, the eventual reduction in gross investment would be approximately as large as the increase in tax revenue that would result from the proposed changes in corporate tax rules. To state this conclusion in different words, the estimates imply that the increased tax revenue would eventually come entirely at the expense of reduced investment.

Martin Feldstein is the George F. Baker Professor of Economics at Harvard University and the president of the National Bureau of Economic Research.
    1. The evidence is presented in Feldstein and Jun (1987).

Statistical analysis of the effects of taxation on investment is, of course, made difficult by the complexity of the investment process. Individual corporate investment decisions reflect a myriad of considerations. In addition to tax rules and financing costs, individual investment decisions respond to technological changes, market opportunities, capacity utilization pressures, and long-term corporate strategies. No statistical model can begin to incorporate all of these complexities.

My own strategy of research in this area therefore has been to focus on aggregate investment and to study several alternative simple models that "let the data speak for themselves." Looking at total business investment rather than the specific investments of individual firms or industries minimizes the importance of the very specific (and generally unobservable) factors that influence particular investment decisions. Although particular industries or types of investment may be unusually strong at a certain time, this will generally be balanced within the overall aggregate by other investments that are relatively weak. Thus oil industry investments may be depressed at the present time, but investments in industries that compete with foreign imports are likely to become relatively strong because of the recent decline in the dollar. Similarly, while computer-related investments were relatively strong in the first half of the 1980s, this was balanced by the unusually weak activity in those industries that were then hurt by the very strong dollar. These specific factors tend to be submerged in the overall aggregate level of investment, which responds to factors that are common to most industries and most types of investments.

Studying alternative simple specifications provides a way of judging whether the estimates are robust to what is inevitably a substantial simplification. The statistical analysis summarized in this paper considers two ways of measuring the impact on business investment of tax-induced changes in profitability. The first method relates investment to the net of tax profitability of existing corporate capital. The second method relates investment to the difference between the after-tax profitability of new investments and the cost of debt and equity capital to the firm. Although the two methods are conceptually and operationally quite different, they provide similar estimates of the effect on investment of changing tax rules.

The analysis discussed in this paper deals with the ratio of net nonresidential fixed investment to GNP. Nonresidential fixed investment is the investment that corporations and noncorporate businesses make in plant and equipment. Every type of nonfinancial investment other than inventories and land is included. In 1985, nonresidential fixed investment was approximately $475 billion. The Department of Commerce estimates that nearly three-fourths of this amount was required to replace the capital stock that is lost through actual depreciation during the year. Thus net nonresidential fixed investment was $133 billion.

Table 6.1 presents data on the ratios of investment to GNP since 1955.[2] The distinction between gross and net investment is clearly important. The ratio of gross investment to GNP has been rising since the mid-1960s, even though the net investment ratio declined by nearly one-third over that same period. The reason for this difference is that economic depreciation (i.e., the difference between gross and net investment) as a share of GNP has been rising. This increase in relative depreciation has occurred for three reasons: the size of the capital stock rose relative to GNP, the share of equipment in the capital stock rose (which raises depreciation because equipment depreciates more rapidly than structures), and the nature of the equipment shifted to more rapidly depreciating types of assets such as computers.

Net investment is the economically important concept because it is net investment that determines the growth of the nation's capital stock. Moreover, a change in net investment eventually causes a corresponding change in the total capital stock and thus in both depreciation and

Table 6.1   **Ratios of Investment to GNP**

Years	Net Investment	Gross Investment
1955–59	.026	.093
1960–64	.025	.091
1965–69	.042	.106
1970–74	.034	.105
1975–79	.027	.104
1980–84	.029	.115
1979	.037	.115
1980	.030	.112
1981	.032	.116
1982	.023	.113
1983	.022	.111
1984	.037	.125
1985[a]	.040	.130

[a]Data for 1985 refer to the first three quarters only at a seasonally adjusted annual rate.

2. The data in table 6.1 and all other data presented and used in this paper are based on the national income and product accounts (NIPA) available in the fall of 1985 when the research was completed. The December 1985 benchmark revisions of the national income and product accounts are not reflected in any of the current analysis since information on the net capital stock, net investment, and other key variables was not available by the end of 1985. The data for 1985 refer to only the first three quarters of the year since data for the fourth quarter are not available on the old NIPA basis.

gross investment. Therefore, the analysis in this paper focuses on net investment.

The data in table 6.1 show that net nonresidential fixed investment has averaged only 3.0% of GNP during the three decades from 1955 through 1984. The period began with investment at an even lower level of only about 2.5% of GNP, a condition that contributed to the Kennedy tax bill and the introduction of the investment tax credit. Net investment rose to over 4% of GNP in the second half of the 1960s (reaching a peak of 4.7% in 1966) and then declined to 3.4% of GNP in the first half of the 1970s and only 2.7% of GNP in the second half of the decade. In the 1980s, investment was initially just slightly above 3% of GNP, then declined during 1982 and 1983 to only 2.2% of GNP before rising to 3.7% in 1984 and 4.0% in 1985. At 4.0% of GNP, the 1985 level of net investment was only exceeded in four other years during the past three decades and always at a time when the level of capacity utilization was substantially higher than it was in 1985.

6.1 Investment and the Net Rate of Return

One way of assessing the impact of tax rules on investment is to examine the relationship between investment and the real net-of-tax rate of return earned on the capital invested in the nonfinancial corporate sector. Table 6.2 presents data on the ratio of net nonresidential

Table 6.2   **The Rate of Investment and the Net Rate of Return**

Year[a]	Investment-GNP Ratio (1)	Net Rate of Return (2)	Capacity Utilization (3)
1955–59	.026	.033	.824
1960–64	.025	.042	.808
1965–69	.042	.060	.080
1970–74	.034	.037	.826
1975–79	.027	.028	.796
1980–84	.029	.029	.773
1979	.037	.032	.842
1980	.030	.026	.846
1981	.032	.019	.793
1982	.023	.029	.783
1983	.022	.030	.703
1984	.037	.041	.740
1985[b]	.040	.054	.808

[a]All variables in col. 2 and 3 are lagged one year. Thus, capacity utilization 1965–69 refers to average capacity utilization in 1964–68.

[b]Investment for 1985 refers to the first three quarters at a seasonally adjusted rate.

fixed investment to GNP (col. 1), the net-of-tax return on nonfinancial corporate capital (col. 2), and the rate of capacity utilization (col. 3). Since statistical studies generally indicate that there is a lag of twelve to eighteen months in the response of investment to changes in its determinants, rate of return and capacity utilization in table 6.2 are shown with a one-year lag; thus capacity utilization for 1955–59 actually refers to the average capacity utilization rate in the period 1954–58.

The starting point for calculating the net-of-tax rate of return variable is the pretax return on nonfinancial corporate capital. Joosung Jun and I constructed this measure as the ratio of profits (with economic depreciation and an inventory evaluation adjustment) plus net interest payments to the value of the corresponding corporate capital stock at replacement cost. To obtain the net rate of return, shown in column 2, we subtract from this the ratio to the capital stock of the taxes paid by the corporations, their shareholders, and their creditors to federal, state, and local governments.[3] Thus, the net rate of return reflects variations in the pretax profitability of capital and in the overall effective tax rate.

A high value of the net return on nonfinancial corporate capital should make this type of investment more attractive relative to other potential uses of funds such as owner-occupied housing, government debt, real estate syndications, and overseas investment. A comparison of columns 1 and 2 shows that there has been a strong association between the variations in this net return and the concurrent variations in the ratio of investment to GNP. The net rate of return was highest in the second half of the 1960s (6.0%) when the investment-GNP ratio was highest (4.2%) and lowest in the second half of the 1970s (2.8%) when the investment-GNP ratio was lowest (2.7%). During the first half of the 1980s, the annual values of the net rate of return rose to a quite strong 5.4%, roughly paralleling the rise in the investment-GNP ratio to 4.0%.

Virtually all of the increase in the net rate of return since the late 1970s has resulted from tax legislation and from the reduction in the rate of inflation. The fall in inflation has been important because the high inflation rate of the late 1970s increased effective tax rates by eroding the value of depreciation and producing artificial capital gains. The pretax real rate of return fluctuated from year to year but was essentially the same in 1983–84 as it had been five years earlier.

One reason for the year-to-year variations in profitability is the cyclical fluctuation in capacity utilization shown in column 3. Such cyclical fluctuations in capacity utilization are also a direct and inde-

3. A complete description of this calculation is presented in Feldstein and Jun (1986).

pendent cause of variations in investment activity. The statistical models that I have estimated allow for the separate effects of net profitability and of capacity utilization. These statistical models, described fully in Feldstein and Jun (1986), show that the combination of the real net rate of return and the rate of capacity utilization explains most of the year-to-year variation in the ratio of net investment to GNP. Figure 6.1 shows the actual annual ratios of net investment to GNP (the solid line) and the value predicted by a model that relates the investment-GNP ratio to the net profitability of column 2 and the capacity utilization of column 3 in table 6.2 (the broken line).

What is particularly important is the statistical evidence that there is a strong and independent relation between investment and the real net rate of return of the previous year. A typical example of the estimated relation implies that each one-percentage-point increase in the real net rate of return on nonfinancial corporate capital raises the investment-GNP ratio by 0.4 percentage points.

Although this can only approximate an average relationship over the entire thirty-year period, it is interesting to note how well it explains major shifts in the investment ratio. Consider, for example, the sharp fall in investment between the high of 4.2% of GNP in 1965–69 and the 2.7% of GNP a decade later, a decline of 1.5% of GNP. Between these same dates, the net return fell from 6.0% to 2.8%, a fall of 3.2%. Applying the overall estimate that each percentage point change in the rate of return alters the investment ratio by 0.4 percentage points im-

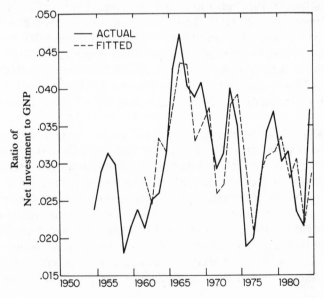

Fig. 6.1   Return over cost model

plies a decline in the investment-GNP ratio of 1.3 percentage points. Thus the decline in the rate of return between the late 1960s and the late 1970s can account for more than 85% of the fall in the investment-GNP ratio.

The predictions of the net return analysis also fit well with the experience of the 1980s. The investment-GNP ratio rose from 3.3% in 1979–81 to 3.9% in 1984–85, an increase of nearly 20%. The corresponding lagged measures of the real net rate of return rose from 2.6% to 4.8%, implying a 0.9-percentage-point rise in the investment-GNP ratio, while the decline in capacity utilization implied a 0.1-percentage-point fall in the investment-GNP ratio. Thus the actual increase in investment was slightly less than the increase predicted on the basis of the stronger investment incentive implied by the sharp rise in the real net rate of return.

The analysis also provides a basis for making a rough calculation of how investment would respond to future changes in tax rules such as those proposed by the administration in May 1985 or the ones enacted by the House of Representatives in December 1985. The administration's proposal would raise corporate tax liabilities by about 25%. The proportional decrease in personal taxes on capital income would be much smaller. The relation between investment and the real net rate of return implies that the administration plan would reduce the investment-GNP ratio by about 4% of its average over the past three decades.

Over time, the lower net investment would mean a smaller capital stock and therefore lower replacement investment as well. In the end, gross investment would be reduced by somewhat more than 4% of what it would be under current law. At the 1988 level of GNP, this would be equivalent to a reduction of $20–$25 billion in gross investment, just about the amount of revenue that would be raised by the net increase in the taxation of capital. In short, the ultimate effect of the proposed tax change would be to reduce gross investment by an amount equal to the rise in the tax on capital. All of the increased revenue would come out of reduced investment.

The tax plan passed by the House of Representatives would eventually raise corporate taxes by about twice as much as the administration plan. Its effect would therefore be to reduce investment by about twice as much as the administration plan. Again, the analysis implies that all of the increased revenue would eventually come out of reduced investment.

6.2   Profitability and the Cost of Capital

As I emphasized at the beginning of this paper, any economic model represents a substantial simplification and, as such, can lead to incorrect inferences. The only way to draw reliable inferences is to use a variety of alternative models that involve different simplifying assumptions. If the different approaches lead to the same conclusion, that conclusion can be held with greater confidence.

With this in mind, I have related the investment-GNP ratio to the difference between corporate profitability and the cost of funds. More specifically, I measured after-tax corporate profitability by the maximum real net return that corporations can afford to pay to providers of debt and equity capital for funds invested in a "standard investment" in plant and equipment. This measure of profitability is altered by changes in tax rules (the corporate and personal tax rates, depreciation schedules, and the investment tax credit) and by changes in projected inflation. Column 2 of table 6.3 shows the behavior of this profitability measure since 1961.

The incentive to invest depends on the difference between the net profitability of investment and the actual cost of funds to corporations, that is, the real net-of-tax returns that the firm must pay on debt and equity capital. Column 3 of table 6.3 presents the calculated values of the real cost of funds since 1961.

The potential real net return was quite high in the mid-1960s (reaching 6.7%), was eroded by the interaction of inflation and depreciation rules in the 1970s, and then rose sharply after passage of the 1981 Economic Recovery Tax Act. Although the real cost of funds was also substan-

Table 6.3   **The Rate of Investment and the Net Rate of Return over Cost**

Year[a]	Investment-GNP Ratio (1)	Maximum Potential Real Net Return (2)	Real Cost of Funds (3)	Maximum Potential Return Minus Cost of Funds (4)
1961–64	.026	.050	.033	.017
1965–69	.042	.059	.041	.018
1970–74	.034	.051	.036	.015
1975–79	.027	.056	.040	.016
1980–84	.029	.068	.050	.018
1979	.037	.059	.052	.007
1980	.030	.061	.053	.008
1981	.032	.059	.047	.012
1982	.023	.072	.053	.019
1983	.022	.075	.053	.022
1984	.037	.075	.046	.029
1985[b]	.040	.073	.060	.013

[a]All variables in col. 2–4 are lagged one year. Thus, capacity utilization 1965–69 refers to average capacity utilization in 1964–68.

[b]Investment for 1985 refers to the first three quarters at a seasonally adjusted rate.

tially higher in recent years than it had been before, the difference between the potential real return on investments in plant and equipment and the cost of funds for those investments (presented in col. 4 of table 6.3) doubled between the final years of the 1970s and the first three years after the 1981 legislation.

My statistical analysis with Joosung Jun shows that each one-percentage-point increase in the difference between the real net return and the cost of funds raises the investment-GNP ratio by about 0.3 percentage points. This estimate implies that the increase in the difference between the real net return and the cost of funds since the beginning of the decade can account for about two-thirds of the rise in investment since that date. In short, this model, like the previous one, indicates a very substantial effect of the changing tax rules on the incentive to invest in plant and equipment. Figure 6.2 compares the actual investment-GNP ratio with the ratios predicted by a combination of the capacity utilization rate and the difference between profitability and the cost of funds.

The administration's 1985 tax proposal would reduce the potential net return on equipment quite substantially and raise the net return on structures. On balance, the potential net return on the average combination of plant and equipment would decline only slightly, implying a relatively modest reduction in the overall investment-GNP ratio (although probably a quite substantial effect on equipment investment).

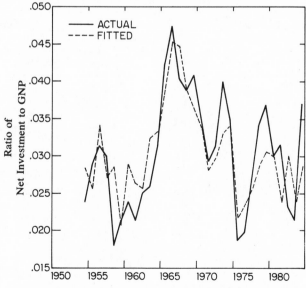

Fig. 6.2   Net return model

In contrast to this small effect of the administration's tax proposal, the House bill implies that the potential real net return would fall by 1.4 percentage points, about 20% of its current value. Our statistical analysis implies that this would reduce the ratio of net investment to GNP by about 0.4% of GNP or some 15% of its three-decade average. This implies that the near-term reduction in investment would be equal to about half of the increase in corporate tax revenue. The resulting decline in the growth of the capital stock would eventually reduce gross investment by 15%, an amount equal to some 1.5% of GNP or 50% more than the increased revenue that would result from the House bill's proposed increase in corporate taxes. In other words, the eventual effect of the House bill would be to reduce fixed nonresidential investment by $1.50 for every dollar of additional tax revenue collected from businesses.

Reference

Feldstein, Martin, and Joosung Jun. 1987. The effects of tax rules on nonresidential fixed investment: Some preliminary evidence from the 1980s. NBER Working Paper 1857. In *The effects of taxation on capital accumulation,* ed. Martin Feldstein. Chicago: University of Chicago Press, 1987.

7 Tax Policy and the International Location of Investment

Michael J. Boskin

7.1 Introduction

Foreign direct investment (FDI) in the United States and U.S. direct investment abroad (DIA) are both important economic phenomena and a source of political controversy. In 1980, FDI reached $17 billion, about 22% as large as net domestic fixed investment. Correspondingly, DIA reached $19 billion, about 25% as large as net domestic investment in plant and equipment. Since 1980, there has continued to be substantial FDI, but DIA has fallen precipitously. Further, the sources of finance for FDI and the uses of earnings on DIA have changed dramatically in the past few years.

Tax policy has therefore become concerned with these flows, in both directions. For example, the Accelerated Cost Recovery System (ACRS), adopted in 1981 and amended in 1982, was limited expressly to investment in the United States. The primary motivation behind ACRS was to increase U.S. domestic capital formation, but a secondary concern, evidenced in the hearings preceding its adoption, was to stem the flow of U.S. investment abroad.

Further, FDI is often seen as an important justification for continuing the U.S. corporate income tax, even among those who favor corporate and personal tax integration. Another policy relevant to revenue (and perhaps location of investment) was the per-country limitation to the foreign tax credit in the administration's tax reform proposal.

There are undoubtedly a wide variety of reasons for multinational firms to invest outside of their home country: access to markets, political considerations, labor costs, proximity to suppliers, and expected

Michael J. Boskin is a professor of economics at Stanford University and a research associate of the National Bureau of Economic Research.

economic conditions, to name a few. Often, the reasons may be specific to an industry, firm, or even a product. In addition to these other forces shaping the international location, tax laws also potentially affect the attractiveness of U.S. direct investment abroad and of foreign direct investment in the United States, as well as the repatriation of earnings and/or capital. The major changes in incentives for U.S. domestic investment enacted in 1981 and 1982 (ERTA and TEFRA, respectively), combined with the trends in FDI and DIA and the current tax reform proposals that might substantially affect tax rates on DIA and FDI, lead me to reexamine the extent to which tax policy influences the international location of investment.

In section 7.2, I begin with a brief review of the literature. Section 7.3 discusses definitions and trends in the data. My results are presented in section 7.4. Section 7.5 then applies these results to the 1981–82 tax changes and discusses the welfare effects of tax policy.

7.2   A Brief Review of the Literature

Domestic tax policy affects the international location of investment primarily through two channels: the home country's tax policy toward investment located there and its tax policy toward foreign source income.

Domestic tax policy on investments made in the home country affect both FDI at home and DIA by home country firms, because tax policy alters the relative rates of return available at home and abroad. Entrepreneurs investing capital will naturally be attracted to locations where the (risk-adjusted) rate of return is highest. Of course, this channel hinges on the substitutability of foreign and domestic investment for a firm. However, the common conception of foreign and domestic investment as alternative methods of producing the same good and/or serving the same (geographic) market suggests that there is some substitution between locations of investment. Thus, there are good theoretical reasons for domestic tax policy to affect both FDI and DIA through its impact on relative rates of return.

The importance of taxes on foreign source income has long been a subject of debate. There are two major approaches to taxation of foreign source income. In the "territorial" approach, the company pays no home country taxes on foreign income. In the "residence" approach, the company does pay home country taxes, but often a credit or deduction is allowed for taxes paid in the host country. The United States uses the residence approach and allows a credit for taxes paid to other countries.

David Hartman (1981, 1984, 1985) has pointed out that, contrary to popular wisdom, the taxation of foreign source income may not affect the international location of investment very much. Hartman properly draws attention to the distinction between investment financed out of retained earnings abroad and investment financed by transfers from home. If the subsidiary is investing out of retained earnings, then the home country tax on foreign source income does not affect the marginal investment decision, because the repatriation of earnings, not the earnings themselves, are the tax base. The home country tax on foreign source income is unavoidable, and its present value does not depend on the length of deferral. Thus, the marginal investment decision for investment out of retained earnings should depend only on net returns available in the home country or the host country.

For firms that finance foreign investment by transfers from home, the home country tax on foreign source income does matter because no foreign earnings have accrued. Thus, the tax on foreign source income is avoidable. One implication of this theory is that a foreign affiliate should never simultaneously repatriate earnings and draw funds from home, since this creates a completely avoidable tax liability. Hartman defines firms that finance foreign investment by retention of earnings as "mature" firms and those that finance investment by transfers from home as "immature." He argues that a large part of U.S. DIA is undertaken by mature firms, since approximately 70% of DIA in 1975–79 was financed by retained earnings. In recent years DIA financed by retained earnings has risen even further. Thus, the U.S. tax on foreign source income may not affect DIA to any great extent. However, if major revisions in tax policy occur frequently (as has been the case), then a firm will have an incentive to wait for lower rates, so the theory may not hold exactly.

7.3 Data

7.3.1 Introduction

Foreign direct investment refers to the infusion of funds into a U.S. subsidiary by the foreign parent or to the retention of earnings by that subsidiary.[1] U.S. direct investment abroad is defined equivalently for the foreign subsidiaries of U.S. parent companies.

Two aspects of this definition merit comment. First, FDI and DIA are not necessarily the dominant aspects of international capital flows. As of the end of 1983, FDI in the United States equaled approximately

---

1. The Bureau of Economic Analysis defines a U.S. affiliate as "a U.S. business enterprise in which a foreign person owns or controls, directly or indirectly, at least 10 percent of the voting securities of an incorporated U.S. business enterprise or an equivalent interest in an unincorporated business enterprise." See U.S. Department of Commerce 1980, 2.

18% of all foreign assets in the United States, while U.S. DIA represented 25% of U.S. assets abroad (Scholl 1985).

Second, FDI and DIA are not exact counterparts to domestic net investment figures. For example, inflows of funds (or retention of earnings) are not necessarily used to purchase real capital assets, so FDI may overstate real foreign net investment. On the other hand, U.S. borrowing by the U.S. subsidiary is not part of the calculation of FDI. Nevertheless, Hartman (1981, 1984) suggests that it is reasonable to use direct investment numbers as net investment.

7.3.2   Trends

Table 7.1 presents summary data on trends in FDI and DIA.[2] Foreign direct investment has grown 2,000% in real terms from 1950 to 1984. Large swings characterize the last third of this period, with tremendous growth from 1977 to 1981, a collapse of 50% in 1982 and 1983, and a doubling in 1984. The FDI figures are also large in relative terms. In every year since 1980, FDI has been more than 20% of U.S. nonresidential net investment in plant and equipment. This is especially noteworthy for 1984, because net investment in the United States rose by over 100% of its 1983 level. The composition of the sources of FDI has also changed over time. Since 1977, the percentage of FDI financed by retained earnings has fallen substantially. This has occurred contemporaneously with the large rise in FDI documented in column 1,

Table 7.1   **Foreign Direct Investment and Direct Investment Abroad: Selected Years, 1950–84 (Current $ Millions)**

Year	FDI	DIA
1950	270	1,096
1960	315	2,941
1970	1,464	7,589
1979	11,876	25,222
1980	16,918	19,222
1981	25,195	9,624
1982	13,792	−4,424[a]
1983	11,946	5,394
1984	22,514	4,503

Sources: U.S. Department of Commerce (1983, 1984); and various issues of the *Survey of Current Business*.

Note: For calculation of real FDI and DIA, cited in the text, note that the GNP deflator in 1950 = 53.5; in 1984 = 223.4.

[a]In 1982, DIA financed by retained earnings was positive, but U.S. affiliates abroad transferred home more funds, so net DIA was negative.

2. All data on FDI and DIA have been obtained from U.S. Department of Commerce (1983, 1984) or selected issues of the *Survey of Current Business*.

thus suggesting that investment financed by intercompany debt and equity flows has dominated FDI for recent years.

U.S. direct investment abroad grew steadily through 1979 but has since collapsed, representing a large and continuing repatriation of funds to the United States. Real DIA in 1984 was only 2% higher than it was in 1950. These observations are reinforced by examination of DIA as a percentage of U.S. nonresidential net investment. The DIA was consistently 20% or more of net investment in the 1960s and 1970s but has collapsed to 11% or less since 1981.

As of the end of 1984, the positions (net capital stocks) in FDI and DIA were $159 billion and $235 billion, respectively. Approximately one-third of the FDI position is in manufacturing and one-sixth is in petroleum. These two industries also account for 40% and 25% of the DIA position, respectively. Not surprisingly, European countries represent the largest share of both positions. Although Japan accounts for only 9.3% of the FDI position, this figure has risen from 2.1% in 1975 and 6.4% in 1979, it should be noted. Moreover, as mentioned earlier, capital inflows may occur predominantly in forms other than FDI.

Thus, even a cursory examination of the data suggests that both FDI and DIA can be substantial. The wide swings further suggest that international investment flows may be very sensitive to current or anticipated conditions.

7.4 Results

My study of FDI and DIA uses alternative sample periods, functional forms, and sets of explanatory variables. In each case, because of the theoretical considerations discussed, I separately analyze investments financed by retained earnings and investments financed by intercompany transfers of debt and equity. Sample periods are 1965–79, 1965–84, and 1956–84. To ensure comparability with other studies, I focus on estimates of FDI and DIA as a proportion of GNP. The main explanatory variables are rates of return and tax rates here and abroad.[3] Other variables are also used, such as adjusted output and measures that control for the energy price rises in the 1970s, but they turn out not to affect the results very much.

In general, the results indicate that tax policy can have an important effect on the international location of investment. Here are presented some examples for 1965–79. A fuller analysis and accompanying discussion are presented in Boskin and Gale (1987).

The results indicate that FDI financed by retained earnings is quite responsive to the return on FDI. A 10% rise in the return (e.g., from

---

3. All tax-rate and rate-of-return data have been obtained from Feldstein and Jun (1987). Further details on data issues are presented in Boskin and Gale (1987).

10% to 11%) increases annual FDI by about 14%, corresponding to an elasticity of 1.4.[4] The elasticity with respect to foreigners' average return in the United States is about 0.9.[5] FDI financed by transfers is less sensitive to the return on FDI but slightly more sensitive to variations in foreigners' average return in the United States.[6]

DIA is very sensitive to the net rate of return on DIA.[7] It is also moderately sensitive to variations in the net return available in the United States.[8] These results hold up under the alternative specifications. They indicate that a 10% rise in the return on DIA (e.g., from 10% to 11%) increases annual DIA by 12%; a 10% rise in the return available in the United States decreases DIA by about 2%.

7.5 Summary and Implications

I have presented new evidence that U.S. domestic tax policy affects the international location of investment. While the results are somewhat sensitive to the sample period, functional form, and other considerations, the qualitative conclusions tend to hold up well. Two empirical issues are particularly interesting: the likely impact of the 1981–82 corporate tax changes on FDI and DIA and the corresponding potential effects of any corporate tax reform. However, the welfare aspects of the international location of investment are also important.

My estimates of the impact on DIA of changes in the after-tax rate of return in the United States suggest that for every dollar of increased U.S. domestic investment, there is a reduction of approximately four cents of DIA. This estimate comes from a comparison of analogous coefficients on domestic investment equations estimated by Feldstein and Jun (1986). It refers only to investment out of retained earnings. Transfers from domestic parent companies to foreign subsidiaries, or the establishment of such subsidiaries, are also likely to respond to domestic tax policy, but the data are insufficient to reach any specific conclusions on that matter.

I estimate that a tax policy that raises the after-tax rate of return enough to lead to a dollar of increased domestic investment in the United States brings with it between eight and twenty-seven cents of FDI. These results are consistent with Hartman's (1981, 1984).

4. This elasticity is estimated to be 1.0 in equations using alternative sample periods. The return on FDI is calculated as FDI income divided by the FDI position.

5. In other sample periods, this elasticity varies substantially, but averages about 1.2. Foreigners' average return in the United States is the overall rate of return in the United States multiplied by one minus the tax rate paid at the corporate level.

6. Alternative functional forms and explanatory variables lead to the same qualitative conclusions.

7. The return on DIA is calculated as DIA income divided by the DIA position.

8. The net return in the United States is the overall rate of return multiplied by one minus the total effective tax rate.

Several studies have analyzed the effect of the 1981–82 investment incentives on effective marginal tax rates (e.g., see Auerbach 1983; Feldstein and Jun 1987; Gravelle 1983; or Hulten and Robertson 1983). These studies generally find that the effective corporate tax rate was reduced by about 20%–35%. With a constant before-tax rate of return and a pre-ERTA effective tax rate of about 33%, the tax changes increased foreigners' average net return in the United States by 10%–17%. Other things equal, this change in net return would bring about approximately a 2%–4% decline in DIA and an 11%–20% rise in FDI. This would imply capital inflows of about $0.5–$1.0 billion from smaller DIA and $2–$4 billion in increased FDI. Of course, these figures refer only to FDI and DIA out of retained earnings. Likewise, a tax reform such as HR 3838, which raises (except perhaps at very high inflation rates) the effective tax rate on U.S. corporate investment, would result in an increase in direct investment abroad by U.S. firms and a decrease in FDI in the United States. However, because these results contain no long-term dynamic theory of the optimal international location of investment, they should not be taken as a final guide to the impacts of these tax changes on investment patterns.

Finally, I should address the welfare economics of the international location of investment, described in Caves (1982); Goulder, Shoven, and Whalley (1983); and Hartman (1984). Domestic economic welfare rises with FDI because the United States receives a claim on the rate of return to foreign capital through the taxation of FDI income. Conversely, domestic economic welfare falls when U.S. firms substitute DIA for investment at home, because the nation then receives only the net-of-foreign-tax return (and only when it is repatriated) rather than the gross return. These welfare effects are augmented by the beneficial effects on labor productivity of greater foreign or domestic investment in the United States. Thus, a reduction in taxation of new corporate investment improves welfare through three channels: the standard mechanism, through which lowering the effective marginal tax rate generates new domestic investment opportunities for U.S. firms; a reallocation of the location of investment by U.S. firms toward home and away from abroad; and an increase in FDI. In this paper, we have presented some new evidence that these last two effects are quantitatively important and therefore that it is necessary to consider them in any evaluation of domestic investment incentives.

The welfare effects of tax policy clearly depend on the responsiveness of FDI and DIA to net-of-tax returns. The welfare gains to a tax reduction on new corporate investment in the U.S. are positively linked to the responsiveness of DIA and FDI with respect to net-of-tax returns in the United States.

My results suggest that accelerated depreciation or tax credits for *new* investment, which decrease the effective marginal tax rate paid at the corporate level by 10%, would raise FDI by 9% through their effect on the net-of-tax return available to FDI. Corporate tax revenues from the taxation of FDI could be expected to rise correspondingly. Similar, though smaller, revenue effects would occur for DIA. These results refer only to investment financed by retained earnings. However, tax revenue is greater per dollar of potential DIA diverted to domestic investment than per dollar of FDI, because foreign owners of U.S. capital pay taxes only at the corporate level, while domestic owners are also responsible for state, local, and personal taxes.

My results suggest that the tax effects on the international location of investments are important. Tax policies such as ACRS and ITC, which raise the after-tax rate of return on new investment without losing revenue from previous investment, not only stimulate domestic fixed investment but also attract additional investment from abroad. The additional investment supplements the impact of domestic investment on productivity and raises corporate tax revenue. However, my results should be taken as preliminary estimates, not as definitive statements about the long-run impacts of tax policy.

References

Auerbach, Alan J. 1983. Corporate taxation in the United States. *Brookings Papers on Economic Activity,* no. 2, pp. 451–505.

Belli, David R. 1984. Foreign direct investment in the United States in 1983. *Survey of Current Business* (October), p. 34.

Boskin, Michael J., and William G. Gale. 1987. New results on the effects of tax policy on the international location of investment. NBER Working Paper 1862. In *The effects of taxation on capital accumulation,* ed. Martin Feldstein. Chicago: University of Chicago Press.

Caves, Richard. 1982. Multinational enterprise and economic analysis. *Cambridge surveys of economic literature.* Cambridge: Cambridge University Press.

Feldstein, Martin, and Joosung Jun. 1987. The effects of tax rules on nonresidential fixed investment: Some preliminary evidence from the 1980s. In *The effects of taxation on capital accumulation,* ed. Martin Feldstein. Chicago: University of Chicago Press.

Goulder, Lawrence H., John B. Shoven, and John Whalley. 1983. Domestic tax policy and the foreign sector: The importance of alternative foreign sector formulations to results from a general equilibrium tax analysis model. In *Behavioral simulations in tax policy analysis,* ed. Martin Feldstein, pp. 333–67. Chicago: University of Chicago Press.

Gravelle, Jane G. 1983. Capital income taxation and efficiency in the allocation of investment. *National Tax Journal,* pp. 297–306.

Hartman, David G. 1981. Domestic tax policy and foreign investment: Some evidence. NBER Working Paper 784. Cambridge, Mass.: National Bureau of Economic Research.

————. 1984. Tax policy and foreign direct investment in the United States. *National Tax Journal* 37:475–87.

————. 1985. Tax policy and foreign direct investment. *Journal of Public Economics* 26:107–21.

Hulten, C., and J. Robertson. 1983. Corporate tax policy and economic growth: An analysis of the 1981 and 1982 tax acts. Washington, D.C.: Urban Institute Press.

Scholl, Russell B. 1985. The international investment position of the United States in 1984. *Survey of Current Business* (June).

Survey of Current Business. Various issues.

U.S. Department of Commerce. 1980. *Foreign direct investment in the U.S.*

————. 1983. *Selected data on U.S. direct investment abroad, 1950–76.*

————. Bureau of Economic Analysis. 1984. *Selected data on foreign direct investment in the United States, 1950–79.*

II Summaries of Additional Studies

8 Anticipated Tax Changes and the Timing of Investment

Alan J. Auerbach and James R. Hines, Jr.

Important changes in the federal tax provisions affecting investment in business plant and equipment were enacted in 1982, 1984, and 1985. There is every reason to believe that 1986 will not be an exception to this pattern. Yet the methods economists use to measure the impacts of changes in the tax law generally assume that such changes will be permanent; they ignore problems of transition. Such analysis can be valuable for understanding the underlying differences among alternative tax systems but may be uninformative about the short-run impact of tax reform on investment. Moreover, the effects of tax changes on the value of corporate securities is typically ignored, although the effects may be quite large.

Consideration of short-run effects on investment and market value requires a careful analysis of three elements of behavior that are normally omitted from long-run analysis of tax reforms: the state of investor expectations, the time lags involved in putting new capital in place, and the tax law's distinctions between new and old capital. Continual tax changes that may appear beneficial when examined in isolation have the potential to be destabilizing when used in combination and when anticipated by investors. To the extent that businesses require time to adjust to changing economic conditions, attempts at frequent fine-tuning of the tax system may do little more than cause the stock market to fluctuate. Additional changes in market value may be associated with tax reforms that narrow or widen the gap between the tax benefits available to new and previously purchased assets.

Alan J. Auerbach is a professor of economics at the University of Pennsylvania and a research associate of the National Bureau of Economic Research. James R. Hines, Jr., is an assistant professor of economics and public affairs at the Woodrow Wilson School, Princeton University.

This paper (see Martin Feldstein, ed., *The Effects of Taxation on Capital Accumulation* [Chicago: University of Chicago, 1987]) presents a framework for tax analysis that addresses these issues, focusing on the effects of tax policy on investment and market values over the past three decades and the potential impact of a number of the tax reform plans that have been promulgated in recent months. The model separately considers investment in equipment and investment in plant. The tax law treats these two classes of assets quite differently, and they exhibit different historical investment patterns. The model also allows one to make different assumptions about the degree of investor anticipations of changes in tax policies and other economic conditions. By using parameters based on historical investment patterns, the model allows one to assess realistically the impact of particular policy changes.

Our results for the period 1954–85 suggest that investors did take account of fluctuations in profitability, real interest rates, and the tax code in making their investment plans. Simulations that assume that investors anticipated future changes in these variables produce more realistic annual investment patterns than those that assume all such changes were unanticipated.

This historical period that we study was characterized by generally falling rates of tax on new corporate investment, particularly in equipment. Equipment received major benefits from the introduction of accelerated depreciation in 1954, the investment tax credit in 1962, the Asset Depreciation Range (ADR) System in 1971, and the Accelerated Cost Recovery System (ACRS) in 1981. Over the period, the fixed corporate capital stock grew at a compounded annual rate of 3.9%, with equipment growing at a rate of 5.0% per year, and structures at a rate of 3.1%. It is interesting to ask how much of this growth was due to the tax incentives instituted over the same period.

Our simulations suggest that the investment tax credit alone accounted for a rise of 0.5% per year in the annual growth rate of the equipment capital stock and 0.3% per year for the total fixed capital stock. However, there is also evidence that the timing of the investment tax credit destabilized investment. Equipment investment was extremely strong during the mid-1960s, partly because of the enactment of the credit. Yet our results suggest that investment would have been strong during this period even without the credit, because corporate investors enjoyed very high before-tax profitability of capital during the period. On the other hand, the presence of ACRS during recent years has helped to lessen the observed decline in investment, which we attribute to reduced profitability and extremely high real interest rates. One interesting aspect of the simulations is their inability to explain the strong recovery of 1984 in equipment investment that occurred in the face of continuing low profitability and high real interest rates.

Until the boom of recent years, the poor performance of the stock market had proved a puzzle for economists. At least one reason for the declining real value of the stock market may have been the increasing distinction between the treatment of new and old capital that accompanied incentives for new investment. As a fraction of the corporate fixed capital stock's replacement value, the market value of the corporations themselves should have been about one-third lower in 1985 than in 1954, according to our simulations. This suggests that policies that have been good for investment have not necessarily been good for investors. Investment incentives make new capital more profitable but may reduce the relative value of old capital that lacks comparable tax incentives.

In this light, it is interesting to consider the effects of a variety of proposed tax reforms, including the Bradley-Gephardt "Fair Tax," the Treasury II plan, and the Rostenkowski plan, HR 3838, passed by the House of Representatives in January 1986. Each plan shares three salient characteristics affecting fixed corporate investment: reductions in the corporate tax rate, repeal of the investment tax credit, and a move toward capital recovery allowances based on true economic depreciation. Our simulation results suggest that all three plans would reduce fixed investment in the short run, with the reduction coming primarily in equipment. If the real, after-tax interest rate remains constant, then structures investment is predicted to rise under all three plans in the short run. The investment mix would be similar under the different plans, with the overall level of investment being highest under Treasury II and lowest under the Rostenkowski plan.

Our simulations also predict large windfalls for existing capital assets under all three plans, with Bradley-Gephardt increasing the market value of corporate fixed capital by the most at 26%, and HR 3838 by the least, 16%, again assuming a fixed after-tax interest rate. Thus, all three plans would reverse the trend of the last three decades, when existing assets became less valuable relative to new ones with each new investment incentive. The predicted windfalls result from the reduced corporate tax rate, which applies to new and old income sources alike, and the reduced value of depreciation allowances and investment tax credits available for new investment. They represent a very substantial revenue cost to the Treasury of a magnitude several times larger than would have been recouped by the windfall tax on excess depreciation proposed as part of Treasury II.

9   Tax-Loss Carryforwards and Corporate Tax Incentives

Alan J. Auerbach and James M. Poterba

The recent decline in corporate tax revenues has generated new interest in the corporate income tax. During the last few years, low profitability and highly accelerated depreciation allowances for new investment have combined to generate tax losses for many firms. Some of these firms have been able to carry their losses back against taxes paid in previous years, and they have received refunds. For other firms, however, recent tax losses have exceeded the maximum potential carryback. These firms must carry their unused tax losses forward and use them to offset taxable profits earned in the next fifteen years.

For firms with tax-loss carryforwards, the effective configuration of investment incentives may be substantially different than for fully taxable firms. A firm that is currently taxable and expects to be taxable in the next few years will be able to use its depreciation deductions as soon as they accrue. For a firm with loss carryforwards that does not expect to become taxable in the near future, however, currently accruing depreciation deductions may not be realized for many years. This reduces the effect of investment incentives, such as the investment tax credit or accelerated depreciation allowances. Firms with loss carryforwards also receive a tax benefit, however. Their earnings on new projects may be virtually untaxed for several years, reducing the burden of the corporate tax and therefore encouraging investment.

This paper (see Martin Feldstein, ed., *The Effects of Taxation on Capital Accumulation* [Chicago: University of Chicago Press, 1987]) estimates the importance of loss carryforwards for U.S. firms and then

Alan J. Auerbach is a professor of economics at the University of Pennsylvania and a research associate of the National Bureau of Economic Research. James M. Poterba is an associate professor of economics at the Massachusetts Institute of Technology and a research associate of the National Bureau of Economic Research.

calculates the impact of these carryforwards on corporate investment incentives. We focus on the period 1981–84 and gather data from corporate annual reports and 10-K filings to determine which firms have tax loss carryforwards or are otherwise restricted in their use of investment incentives. We find a substantial increase in the total stock of outstanding loss carryforwards during the sample period, and find that at least 15% of corporations were carrying losses forward at the end of 1984. In some industries, the incidence of loss carryforwards is substantially higher.

To analyze the persistence of loss carryforwards, we estimate the probability that firms with carryforwards will exhaust them and become taxable between one tax year and the next. The data suggest that, between 1982 and 1984, ninety-one out of 100 firms with loss carryforwards in one year continued carrying losses forward in the next year. Only nine out of 100 become fully taxable in a typical year; this suggests that, once a firm experiences a tax-loss carryforward, it may not return to currently taxable status for several years. For taxable firms, the odds of entering the loss-carryforward position are small: only two firms in 100 move from being currently taxable to having a loss carryforward in a typical one-year period. The strong persistence of loss carryforwards makes the deferral of depreciation allowances a potentially significant effect on the firm's investment incentives.

We summarize the effect of loss carryforwards on investment incentives using effective tax rates, which measure the total tax wedge between the pretax and posttax return on investing in different assets. We find that, under pre-1986 law, the effective tax rate for an investment in industrial equipment for a firm that is currently taxable is −5.8%. The negative effective tax rate indicates that the combination of accelerated depreciation and the investment tax credit actually subsidizes equipment investment for taxable firms. For loss-carryforward firms, however, the effective tax rate on equipment is 15.0%. Because these firms are unable to use accelerated depreciation allowances as they accrue, and because they are more likely to be taxable in the distant future when the investment is yielding taxable profits than in the near term when it is generating negative taxable income, the net effect of the tax system discourages these firms from undertaking equipment investments. A rather different picture emerges for the case of industrial buildings, where the taxable and tax-loss firms face similar effective tax rates. For the currently taxable firm, the effective tax rate on buildings is 41.7%, while for the firm with a loss carryforward, it is 38.3%. The tax system provides a net disincentive to structures investment for both classes of firms.

The dramatic disparity in effective tax rates on equipment and the small differences for structures are due to the different time paths of depreciation allowances for the two assets. For equipment, a firm's tax status in the near term is of central importance in determining the present value of its depreciation deductions. For structures, however, the depreciation allowances accrue over a much longer horizon. The fraction of currently taxable firms that will have tax-loss carryforwards ten years from today is much higher than the fraction that will have losses in one year. Similarly, current loss-carryforward firms are more likely to have loss carryforwards again next year than ten years hence. Whether a firm has tax losses today is therefore a better predictor of its tax status during the relevant years for equipment allowances than for structures.

10 Tax Asymmetries and Corporate Income Tax Reform

Saman Majd and Stewart C. Myers

Under current (1985) tax law, corporate income is taxed asymmetrically. Because of the lack of full loss offsets, the government takes more on average from profitable firms than it hands back to nonprofitable ones. Although current losses allow the firm to claim a refund of taxes paid in the three preceding years, once refunds are exhausted, losses must be carried forward to offset future income. The "value per dollar" carried forward is less than the statutory rate for two reasons: (1) the firm may not earn enough to use the carryforwards before they expire, and (2) the carryforwards do not earn interest.

In previous work, we showed that tax asymmetries can be modeled and valued as contingent claims, using option pricing theory combined with Monte Carlo simulation. Tax asymmetries can drastically reduce the after-tax net present values (NPVs) of incremental investment outlays, although the extent of the reduction depends on the tax position of the investing firm and the volatility of its income. The asymmetries are irrelevant for investment by a firm with sufficient other income that it always pays taxes on a marginal dollar of income or loss. But asymmetries may be the dominant tax effect on the value of "stand-alone" projects, that is, in situations where the project and the firm are one and the same.

In this paper (see Martin Feldstein, ed., *The Effects of Taxation on Capital Accumulation* [Chicago: University of Chicago Press, 1987]), we focus on the *design* of the corporate income tax. We report the results of a series of experiments comparing current tax law with a

Saman Majd is an assistant professor of finance at the Wharton School, University of Pennsylvania. Stewart C. Myers is the Gordon Y. Billard Professor of Finance at the Sloan School of Management, Massachusetts Institute of Technology, and a research associate of the National Bureau of Economic Research.

stylized tax reform proposal. The reform reduces the corporate income tax rate to 33% but eliminates the investment tax credit and the ACRS depreciation schedules. Tax depreciation is set approximately equal to economic depreciation over estimated economic asset life. We also investigate the effects of indexing depreciation for inflation.

We find that this type of reform increases the present value of taxes on incremental investments by firms that always pay taxes, but *decreases* the present value of taxes on stand-alone investments, even when depreciation is not indexed for inflation. The additional tax burden due to tax asymmetries is dramatically reduced.

The magnitude of these shifts of course depends on the exact numerical assumptions used in the simulations. However, the direction of the effects holds over a wide range of assumptions about project risk, the rate of economic depreciation, and the ratio of fixed to variable cost.

However, tax reform would not fully eliminate the effects of tax asymmetries. Our experiments generate after-tax NPVs from stand-alone projects under the reformed tax rules that are up to 5% less than the after-tax value of the same investment under symmetric tax. In other words, the asymmetry may allow the government to capture an additional 5% of project investment.

Allowing interest on tax-loss carryforwards is sometimes suggested as a remedy for tax asymmetries. This is a complete solution only if the stand-alone firm or project is certain to regain tax-paying status in the future. If tax-paying status is uncertain, the government's tax option retains value, just as a call option retains value even if its exercise price increases at the interest rate. Thus we find reasonable examples in which less than half of the burden is eliminated.

The burden of tax asymmetries would be completely cancelled out only if the firm could add a life insurance premium as well as interest to unused loss carryforwards. The premium would equal the probability that the firm generating the carryforwards would pass away, taking its carryforwards with it, during the next tax year.

Actual tax reform proposals contain impurities not specifically addressed in our experiments. We point out that our results overstate the difference reform might make because most proposals continue to allow corporations to expense investment in intangibles such as outlays for research and development. The tax shields on investment in intangible assets can be front-loaded in the same way that accelerated depreciation and the investment tax credit front-load the tax benefits of investment in tangible assets. Front-loading helps tax-paying firms but not stand-alone firms or projects lacking immediate income. The riskier that stand-alone firm or project, the more it suffers, because the value of the government's tax option increases as risk increases.

This paper, since it focuses on a particular aspect of the corporate income tax, cannot trace out the full implications of simultaneous changes in corporate and personal income taxes. Nor do we pin down the actual average impact of tax asymmetries under either current or reformed tax rules—only their potential impacts. However, under current law the potential impacts are large enough to make significant distortions plausible. For example, the distortions could reduce the after-tax value of a risky, start-up venture to about 90% of the value of the same venture undertaken by a large, tax-paying firm. Under tax reform, that shortfall could be cut in half.

11   Consumer Spending and the After-Tax Real Interest Rate

N. Gregory Mankiw

The responsiveness of consumer spending to the after-tax real interest rate has important implications for a variety of policy questions. If consumer spending is highly sensitive to the interest rate, then the impact of persistent government deficits on the capital stock is relatively small, since consumers will react to higher deficits by saving more. Understanding the determinants of consumer spending is also necessary before one can evaluate the economic effects of various tax provisions that directly affect the after-tax interest rate. Individual Retirement Accounts (IRAs), for example, serve to lower the tax on capital income and thus to raise the after-tax return to saving. The efficacy of such provisions depends on the responsiveness of consumer spending to the after-tax interest rate.

Despite the importance of this issue, there is little agreement among economists as to how much consumer spending is affected by the after-tax interest rate. Empirical studies have traditionally found that interest rates do not have an important impact on consumer spending. In the past few years, however, several economists have challenged this traditional view on both theoretical and empirical grounds. This paper (see Martin Feldstein, ed., *The Effects of Taxation on Capital Accumulation* [Chicago: University of Chicago Press, 1987]) examines several issues relevant to this debate.

Most previous studies of the interaction between interest rates and consumer spending have ignored, or treated unsatisfactorily, consumer spending on durable goods, such as automobiles, household equipment, and residential structures. This paper examines the interaction between

N. Gregory Mankiw is an assistant professor of economics at Harvard University and a faculty research fellow of the National Bureau of Economic Research.

consumer durable goods and consumer nondurable goods in determining the responsiveness of total expenditure to the after-tax interest rate. It shows how the introduction of durables as part of the consumer's decision affects the interest sensitivity of total spending.

Economic theory suggests that consumer spending on durable goods should be more sensitive to the after-tax interest rate than consumer spending on nondurable goods and services. The channel that makes durable goods more interest sensitive is called the "user cost effect," since the after-tax interest rate is one determinant of the implicit rental cost of consumer durable goods. This paper shows that the user cost of consumer durables indeed affects the composition of consumer spending between durable goods and nondurable goods.

This user cost effect may be one of the most important ways in which the after-tax interest rate affects consumer spending. Previous studies of consumer spending and interest rates have usually examined nondurable consumption in life-cycle models, which assume that individuals have the ability to borrow against their future income if they so choose. Some recent empirical work, however, has cast doubt on the life-cycle hypothesis and has suggested that borrowing constraints play an important role in determining consumer spending. If borrowing constraints are important, then the relevance of the previously studied channels through which the interest rate works is called into question. In contrast, even if an individual cannot borrow against his or her future income, the user cost effect on durable goods makes his or her total spending highly interest sensitive.

Another goal of this paper is to examine the response of various categories of consumer spending to the events of the 1980s. During the early 1980s, policy changes and economic events raised after-tax interest rates to extraordinarily high levels. First, anti-inflationary monetary policy and large government deficits worked to raise market interest rates. At a constant marginal tax rate of 30%, the expected after-tax real interest rate rose from -2.2% in the 1970s to $+0.3\%$ in the early 1980s. Second, reductions in marginal tax rates and increased availability of retirement accounts reduced the effective tax rate on capital income. Third, financial deregulation increased the availability of market interest rates to individuals. For these reasons, after-tax real interest rates were substantially higher in the early 1980s than in the 1970s, suggesting that this episode is an ideal natural experiment to examine the interest sensitivity of consumer spending.

This paper therefore compares consumer spending in the 1980s with the level of spending one would have expected from watching the events of the 1970s. It presents some evidence that the high after-tax real interest rates of the 1980s may have substantially reduced consumer spending on nondurable goods, services, durables, and residential construction. In particular, the evidence is consistent with the implication of economic theory that, because of the user cost effect, spending on consumer durables and residential construction is more highly interest sensitive than is spending on nondurables and services.

Overall, the results of this paper suggest that the after-tax interest rate is indeed an important determinant of consumer spending. Policies that directly alter the after-tax interest rate, such as the availability of IRAs or movements toward expenditure taxation more generally, are therefore likely to have an important impact on saving and thereby on capital formation. Moreover, these policies are also likely to substantially affect the composition of consumer spending between nondurable goods and durable goods.

12 The Impact of Fundamental Tax Reform on the Allocation of Resources

Don Fullerton and Yolanda Kodrzycki Henderson

Recent discussions of tax reform have emphasized the importance of defining the tax base as economic income and of taxing that base at lower rates. Specific proposals have differed with respect to the particular means of implementing these goals. Our paper (see Martin Feldstein, ed., *The Effects of Taxation on Capital Accumulation* [Chicago: University of Chicago Press, 1987]) examines the Treasury tax plan of November 1984 and the president's proposal of May 1985 as they would amend taxation of income from capital. We find that these reforms would differ in their relative emphases on alleviating interasset, intersectoral, interindustry, and intertemporal distortions.

Our approach in this paper is to measure the net effects of proposed changes in statutory rates, credits, depreciation allowances, and other features of the tax code such as the indexation of interest and capital gains. We compare costs of capital for individual assets, sectors, and industries and weight these together to evaluate the impact on total investment incentives under the administration's plans. Then, using a general equilibrium model, we simulate alternative resource allocations and associated changes in welfare.

The results of our study depend in part on the assumed role of dividend taxes. We initially consider the "new view" that dividend taxes have only a small effect on investment incentives. Under this assumption, current law and the president's plan provide the highest incentives for investment as a whole. The costs of capital (and, equivalently, the effective tax rates on income from capital) are similar under these two regimes. The Treasury plan would raise the cost of capital

Don Fullerton is associate professor of economics at the University of Virginia. Yolanda Kodrzycki Henderson is an economist at the Federal Reserve Bank of Boston.

almost 7% from its current level and would therefore tend to deter capital formation. On the other hand, both administration plans would tend to allocate capital more efficiently across its uses. The Treasury plan is most effective in narrowing the disparities in the cost of capital across assets (within each sector). For example, within the corporate sector, we find that the effective rates for investments in different types of equipment, structures, inventories, and land would all lie between 39% and 52%, compared with a range of −4% to +50% under current law. The rates across assets would become more similar because of the abolition of the investment tax credit (which is currently available only for equipment) and because of adoption of depreciation allowances closely adhering to economic depreciation. Remaining differences are primarily the result of differential local property taxes. The president's plan would tax corporate assets at rates ranging from 24% to 45%. This range is larger than under the Treasury plan because of the adoption of accelerated depreciation provisions that confer preferential taxation on depreciable assets relative to inventories and land.

We find, however, that the president's plan would be more effective in narrowing the disparities in capital costs and effective tax rates across industries and sectors than would the Treasury plan. This stems largely from the treatment of corporate investments relative to owner-occupied housing. As a result of elimination of deductibility of local property taxes, both plans would raise somewhat the effective tax rate on owner-occupied housing. The president's plan would not change the overall tax rate in the corporate sector, so the preexisting disparity between corporations and housing is diminished. The Treasury plan would produce a sizable increase in the cost of corporate investments. This increase would lead to a greater difference in the relative treatment of heavily corporate industries such as manufacturing and other industries such as agriculture and housing, where the corporate form of organization is not predominant.

These findings are somewhat changed under the "old view" of dividend taxes. Under this view, dividend taxes are a significant component of capital costs. Corporations would be provided a deduction for 50% of dividends under the Treasury plan and 10% under the president's plan. These features have a more substantial impact on reducing the corporate costs of capital when the old view is considered. Under this theory, we conclude that both plans cause a slight reduction in the overall cost of capital and both would lower intersectoral distortions.

We then turn to a simulation of these reforms over a fifty-year horizon using a general equilibrium model. This model is able to evaluate efficiency gains or losses from the various features of revised taxes on capital incomes. The effect of interasset tax distortions is captured by firms' substitution among different types of equipment, structures, inventories, and land in production in response to their relative capital costs. Intersectoral distortions are captured because of the model's endogenous allocation of capital among corporations, noncorporate business, and owner-occupied housing. Finally, the effect of taxes on intertemporal allocation of resources is captured in that households decide how much to save in response to the after-tax rate of return. This saving determines the accumulation of capital over time.

Under the "new view" of dividend taxes, in most of our simulations, we find that both reforms generate net welfare gains even with slight declines in the capital stock. That is, in terms of output, a more efficient allocation of capital more than makes up for a lower capital stock. Under the "old view" that dividend taxes have a significant effect on investment, both plans reduce intertemporal distortions as well as differences among assets. Under this view, the Treasury plan no longer worsens intertemporal distortions. Even for the least favorable set of parameters in this case, these reforms raise both the capital stock (by 0.5%–0.7%) and the real value of output (by 0.3%–0.4%).

Finally, our paper shows alternative allocations of capital across assets, sectors, and industries. We expect firms to make relatively less use of equipment as a result of the reforms, but the industrial mix of output will depend on the particular assumptions about dividend taxes. Under the Treasury proposal with the new view of dividend taxes, the only industries that would experience a long-run increase in output would be agriculture and housing. Under the president's plan with the new view, more industries would experience increases in output, but housing would decline. Simulation under the old view produces the largest increases in output for the heavily corporate manufacturing and mining industries and declines for real estate.

To summarize, our paper contains a comprehensive model of investment incentives and estimates of the efficiency effects of tax reform. It is important to realize, however, that it does not provide information about the effects of tax reform on equity, simplicity, or other criteria essential to final policy judgments.

13 The Value-added Tax: A General Equilibrium Look at Its Efficiency and Incidence

Charles L. Ballard, John Karl Scholz, and John B. Shoven

A value-added tax (VAT) has been considered repeatedly in the United States either to replace parts of the existing federal tax system or as a new source of revenue to reduce the federal deficit. In this paper (see Martin Feldstein, ed., *The Effects of Taxation on Capital Accumulation* [Chicago: University of Chicago Press, 1987]), we examine the efficiency and distributional consequences of a VAT whose revenues are used to reduce personal or corporate income taxes. In addition to analyzing the VAT as a flat rate tax on consumption, we look at a VAT with a rate structure similar to those prevalent in Europe. In Europe the actual VATs commonly have several rates, exempt housing and most services, tax food lightly, and tax luxuries at the highest rate. We ask how this rate differentiation affects the efficiency of the tax and how effective it is in alleviating the tax's inherent regressivity. As an alternative to rate differentiation, a progressive direct expenditure tax is also evaluated. Such a tax would effectively apply the same rate to all commodities for an individual consumer but would apply higher rates to households with higher levels of expenditure. Finally, the paper examines several ways in which VAT revenues could be used to lower existing taxes. Two possible personal tax reductions are examined, along with replacing the corporate income tax with a VAT.

Our analyses of the tax changes use an applied general equilibrium tax model developed with the support of the U.S. Treasury Department. The model has nineteen industrial sectors, fifteen consumer goods, and twelve classes of households differentiated by their total economic

Charles L. Ballard is an assistant professor of economics at Michigan State University. John Karl Scholz is a graduate student in the Department of Economics, Stanford University. John B. Shoven is a professor of economics at Stanford University and a research associate of the National Bureau of Economic Research.

income in 1973. The model is dynamic in the sense that consumers allocate their income between consumption and saving, and saving determines the growth rate of the capital stock. It incorporates the entire array of existing taxes, including the personal and corporate income taxes, excise and sales taxes, payroll taxes, and property taxes. The analysis involves a comparison of the path of the economy following the introduction of a new tax with the path if the base policy had been retained. In the model, the elasticity of saving with respect to the real after-tax interest rate is set at 0.4, and the elasticity of aggregate labor supply with respect to the real wage rate is set at 0.15. A limited amount of sensitivity analysis is done with respect to the savings elasticity.

The paper finds that the introduction of a VAT and an equal yield reduction in the personal income tax would improve the efficiency of the economy. This is true because those who are made better off by the tax swap would gain more than those who are made worse off. Potentially, the losers could be compensated. The magnitude of the improvement in efficiency is significantly larger for a flat VAT than for one with a differentiated rate structure. For the taxes considered in the paper, rate differentiation costs about $100 billion in present value terms. While this is only 0.2% of the present value of future GNP and leisure simulated in the model, it still is a sizable cost. This $100 billion cost of differentiation implies that the gain from a VAT is reduced 27%–42% by rate differentiation. Relative to a flat rate VAT, a progressive expenditure tax also loses about $100 billion in efficiency. However, all three policies (i.e., a flat VAT, a differentiated VAT, and a progressive expenditure tax) are more efficient at the margin than is the present personal income tax. The magnitude of the efficiency gain depends to a great extent on the manner in which the personal income tax is scaled back. Given that the efficiency losses of taxes vary roughly with the square of the tax rate, reductions that lower the rates are more efficient than reduction for those with lower rates.

Naturally, the manner in which existing taxes are lowered also dramatically affects the incidence of the introduction of a VAT. In fact, the use of the revenue determines the distributional impact of the tax swap more than the design of the VAT's rate structure does. If personal tax rates are reduced proportionally, the tax swap is far more regressive than if they are reduced by a fixed number of percentage points. In fact, the regressivity of the VAT with a fixed percentage-point reduction in personal tax rates is rather mild. We show one case of a progressive expenditure tax with a proportional reduction in personal income tax rates that leaves all income classes better off.

Previous analyses of the integration of the corporation and personal income tax have assumed that the forgone revenues would be made up by an increase in personal income tax rates. In this paper, we examine the possibility of financing the tax integration with the introduction of a VAT. The resulting efficiency gain exceeds previous estimates because a consumption-type VAT is a more efficient source for the needed replacement revenue than a personal income tax surcharge.

To gain a feeling of how important efficiency matters are, we compare four different tax instruments used to raise revenue from households by a given amount: two types of income tax surcharges, a flat VAT, and a differentiated VAT. We find that a percentage income tax surcharge "hurts" households almost 28% more than would the introduction of a flat VAT that raised the same revenue.

Given that a number of the tax swaps considered in the paper involve efficiency improvements but have a regressive incidence, we investigate a range of social welfare functions for which the tax changes offer an improvement. Because reducing income tax rates by a given number of percentage points is more progressive than reducing rates proportionally, use of a VAT's revenue for the first type of reduction leads to an increase in social welfare for a wider range of welfare functions. However, the proportional rate reduction may lead to the larger efficiency gain.

The paper contains some sensitivity analyses with respect to the specification of consumer demands and to saving elasticity. While the numbers obviously change, the qualitative implications of the introduction of a VAT are unaltered.

We conclude that different tax measures impose significantly different efficiency costs on the economy. A flat VAT appears to be far more efficient at the margin than an income tax surcharge. However, rate differentiation is a costly and relatively ineffective way to affect the distribution of welfare in the economy. It would be more effective to change the progressive tax rates of the personal income tax directly (or to introduce a progressive expenditure tax) than to erode the potential efficiency of a value-added tax.

14   The Cash Flow Corporate Income Tax

Mervyn A. King

The current debate on tax reform has raised again the question of what to do about corporate taxation. The cumulative effect of piecemeal changes to the tax system has been to create major distortions to the pattern of savings and investment, and has led to falling revenue in real terms. As a result, the goal of "fiscal neutrality" has attracted a good deal of support from both economists and politicians. The practical expression of this perception of the need for change has been the elimination of many existing concessions to investment and savings. This can be seen most clearly in the major overhaul of the corporate tax system in the United Kingdom in 1984, and in the United States in 1986.

The debate in both countries has focused on moving toward fiscal neutrality by taxing "economic income." The concessions to investment are to be eliminated in return for a cut in the corporate tax rate. But this debate shows that the attempt to return to a comprehensive income tax raises at least as many questions as it answers. The calculation of economic depreciation of an asset is not straightforward, and proposals to index the tax system for inflation have foundered on practical objections. Is there, therefore, any alternative way to attain the objective of fiscal neutrality without a significant erosion of the tax base?

There is indeed such an alternative. It is the *cash flow corporate income tax*. The basic idea is to tax the company on its net cash flow received from real business activities and to avoid any distinction be-

Mervyn A. King is a professor of economics at the London School of Economics and a research associate of the National Bureau of Economic Research.

tween capital and income items. Fiscal neutrality is achieved by harmonizing investment incentives on a common basis of immediate expensing for all assets.

Why not simply abolish corporate income tax altogether? There are two objections. First, a corporate income tax exists already, and to abolish it would be to yield windfall capital gains to the current owners of corporate equity. Second, in the absence of a tax on corporate income, it is not easy for the authorities to tax the income received by either foreign investors in domestic companies or domestic subsidiaries of foreign corporations. The cash flow corporate income tax represents an attempt to construct a tax that is neutral with respect to both financial and investment decisions and at the same time continues to yield the government positive revenue. It requires no adjustment for inflation and hence avoids the complicated indexation provisions that are necessary under alternative tax bases.

The principle of the tax is to levy a charge on the net cash flow to the company resulting from its real economic activities. The tax base is the difference between the receipts from sales of goods and services on the one hand and the purchases of goods and services required in the production process (including purchases of capital goods) on the other hand. This means that no deduction would be allowed for payments to the suppliers of finance. More specifically, this would imply the phasing out of deductibility of interest payments or, alternatively, adding into the tax base new loan capital raised.

The effect of such a tax system would be to increase the incentive to invest in the U.S. economy relative to either the current position or that proposed in the various plans before Congress. At existing tax rates, there would seem to be no reason to suppose that revenue would be lower than current levels. The transitional and administrative problems raised by a switch to the cash flow corporate income tax are discussed in the paper (see Martin Feldstein, ed., *The Effects of Taxation on Capital Accumulation* [Chicago: University of Chicago Press, 1987]), and there appear to be solutions to all of these.

Successful tax reform requires an understanding not only of the effects of the current system but also of alternative systems that can be used as benchmarks to evaluate reform proposals. In this context, the cash flow corporate income tax merits further consideration.

Contributors

Alan J. Auerbach
Economics Department
University of Pennsylvania
3718 Locust Walk/CR
Philadelphia, Pennsylvania 19104

Charles L. Ballard
Department of Economics
Michigan State University
East Lansing, Michigan 48824

Michael J. Boskin
National Bureau of Economic
   Research
204 Junipero Serra Boulevard
Stanford, California 94305

Martin Feldstein
National Bureau of Economic
   Research
1050 Massachusetts Avenue
Cambridge, Massachusetts 02138

Don Fullerton
Department of Economics
Rouss Hall
The University of Virginia
Charlottesville, Virginia 22901

Patric H. Hendershott
Department of Finance
Hagerty Hall
Ohio State University
1775 South College Road
Columbus, Ohio 43210

Yolanda Kodrzycki Henderson
Research Department T-28
Federal Reserve Bank of Boston
600 Atlantic Avenue
Boston, Massachusetts 02106

James R. Hines, Jr.
Woodrow Wilson School
Princeton University
Princeton, New Jersey 08544

Mervyn A. King
London School of Economics
Lionel Robbins Building
Houghton Street
London WC2A 2AE
ENGLAND

Lawrence B. Lindsey
Department of Economics
Harvard University
Littauer Center 231
Cambridge, Massachusetts 02138

Saman Majd
Wharton School
University of Pennsylvania
2300 Steinberg-Dietrich Hall
Philadelphia, Pennsylvania 19104

N. Gregory Mankiw
National Bureau of Economic
    Research
1050 Massachusetts Avenue
Cambridge, Massachusetts 02138

Stewart C. Myers
Sloan School of Management
Massachusetts Institute of
    Technology
50 Memorial Drive
Cambridge, Massachusetts 02139

James M. Poterba
National Bureau of Economic
    Research
1050 Massachusetts Avenue
Cambridge, Massachusetts 02138

John Karl Scholz
Department of Economics
Stanford University
Stanford, California 94305

John B. Shoven
Department of Economics
Stanford University
Stanford, California 94305

Lawrence H. Summers
Department of Economics
Harvard University
Littauer Center 229
Cambridge, Massachusetts 02138

David A. Wise
National Bureau of Economic
    Research
1050 Massachusetts Avenue
Cambridge, Massachusetts 02138

Author Index

113

Subject Index

Accelerated Cost Recovery System (ACRS), 86; elimination of, 94; and international location of investment, 73, 79–80; structures tax treatment since, 37–38, 42, 46, 48

Accelerated depreciation, 86, 102; frontloading of tax incentives through, 33; of structures, 42–46, 48; and tax-loss carryforwards, 89–91

Additional Minimum Tax, 19–21

Administration, tax reform plans of: and allocation of investment resources, 51, 54–56, 58–60, 101–3; and individual retirement account limits, 12–13; and profitability, 63, 69, 71–72

Age, and individual retirement account investment, 6–7, 10–12

Agriculture, 102, 103

Alternative Minimum Tax, 19, 22

Alternative Tax Computation, 19–20

Asset Depreciation Range (ADR), 42, 86

Asymmetries in tax system, 93–95

Borrowing, and consumer spending, 98

Bradley-Gephardt "Fair Tax," 87

Canada, Registered Retirement Savings Plans (RRSPs) in, 4, 9–11, 14

Capacity utilization, 66–68, 71

Capital: distinction between new and old, 85, 87; tax reform and allocation of, 101–3

Capital budgeting theory, 28–30

Capital gains tax, 17–25; and lock-in effect, 17–18; measurement of rates of, 18–22; relationship between realizations, wealth, and rates of, 23–24; on residential property, 48–49; and tax churning, 38, 41–46; and tax reform plans, 54–56; and value of personal assets, 22–23

Capital losses, 17, 19

Cash flow corporation income tax, 109–10

Churning. See Tax churning

Commercial buildings, investment in, 32–33, 38, 42–46

Computers, investments in, 64, 65

Consumer spending, 97–99

Consumption: and individual retirement account limit changes, 12–14; and value-added tax, 105, 106

Corporate investments, 87; and corporate financial policy, 46–47; housing versus, 53, 56, 102–3; patterns of, 39; risk-adjusted rental costs of, 52–60; and tax churning, 43–46; and tax-loss carryforwards, 90

Corporation income taxes: cash-flow, 109–10; and double taxation, 53, 59; fixed investment and reductions in,